RANKING
THE BEST
IN 25 YEARS
OF POP
CULTURE

THE MUST LIST

BY THE EDITORS OF

Entertainment WEEKLY

Contents

Ready to take a trip to the past? Turn to page 4 for the introduction.

Introduction

Hammer pants: not our fault.

When you think about the greatest movies, TV shows, albums, and books of the last 25 years, what makes your list? Nothing inspires more passionate debate at *Entertainment Weekly* than identifying the very best pop culture has to offer, as we do each week in the magazine's The Must List. Now, for *EW*'s 25th anniversary, we offer the absolute Musts of the past quarter-century.

From *Good Will Hunting* to *Breaking Bad*, *X-Men* to *The X-Files*, and from Prince to Queen Latifah to Stephen King, you'll find your favorites here, along with some forgotten gems and new discoveries. And while we expect you may disagree with some of our heartfelt and hard-argued choices, that's the fun of making lists. We'll continue searching out the best in the decades to come in the magazine and on EW.com. But now, get ready for some cultural time travel, starting with…

25 Things We Can't Believe About 1990

1. "U Can't Touch This." MC Hammer revived both Rick James and harem pants with this hip-hop hit. James sued and settled over the "Super Freak" sample; nothing could be done about the pants.

2. We knew K.D. Lang when. The not-yet-mainstream singer's bold mix of musical styles was celebrated on the first cover of *EW* (and later that week, she won her first Grammy, for *Absolute Torch and Twang*).

3. The NC-17 movie rating was created. You're welcome, *Henry & June* and *Showgirls*.

4. "The Wall" live in Berlin. Pink Floyd's Roger Waters and friends performed this rock opera where the Berlin Wall had stood eight months earlier.

5. Andrew Dice Clay on Saturday Night Live. *SNL* used a time delay when the shock comic hosted; Nora Dunn and invited musical guest Sinéad O'Connor boycotted the episode.

6. Roseanne Barr desecrated the national anthem. There were some notes only dogs heard during her performance at a San Diego Padres game.

7. Milli Vanilli, Best New... Lip-Synchers? Nine months after the duo won the Best New Artist Grammy, it was revealed they didn't actually sing.

8. Macaulay Culkin was Home Alone. "Mack is not like a 9-year-old," costar Joe Pesci told *EW* of the kid who carried the comedy to a $476 million worldwide gross. "It's like working with a 30-year-old midget."

9. *Law & Order* **settled in for a 20-year run.** And that iconic "chung-chung" sound? It's a piece of music, composer Mike Post has said, that brings in royalties.

10. *Blue Steel.* The Jamie Lee Curtis thriller was the cover of *EW*'s issue 5. Regrets, we've had a few....

11. Madonna did *Dick Tracy.* But the memorable part of that odd project was her single "Vogue," off the film's companion album, *I'm Breathless.*

12. *Longtime Companion* **put the focus on AIDS.** The first major feature to deal with the crisis, its impact went far beyond its $4.6 million box office gross. Bruce Davison even earned an Oscar nod.

13. *Cheers* **turned 200.** Fans toasted the comedy's bicentennial episode, and by season's end it was the year's top-rated show.

14. "Wind Beneath My Wings" snagged two Grammys. The *Beaches* ballad won Record of the Year and Song of the Year. "We Didn't Start the Fire" must have been too edgy.

15. Save CBS! *EW* mounted a campaign to turn the ailing network around. Twenty-five years later, it's at the top of the heap. Coincidence...?

16. Ah-nold showed his range. The future governor of California excelled in both sci-fi action (*Total Recall*) and comedy (*Kindergarten Cop*).

17. Mariah Carey took the slow road to success. Her debut album took 43 weeks to top the charts, but it was the best-selling album of 1991.

18. *Green Acres* **returned to the tube.** Arnold the pig shined in a reunion movie *EW* deemed "shamelessly hokey" but "affectionate."

19. Oprah grilled the Teenage Mutant Ninja Turtles. "Interspecies relationships" were mentioned. Awkward!

20. We saw the end of the Future. Reflecting on the last *Back to the Future* film, Michael J. Fox told *EW*, "I'm a little older now, and I'm very comfortable about just goofing around."

21. Critics do change their minds—sometimes. In 1990, *EW*'s Owen Gleiberman gave *Pretty Woman* a D for its "plastic screwball soap opera" quality. Twenty years later, he bumped that up to a B, in newfound appreciation of the Richard Gere–Julia Roberts chemistry.

22. Videogames got bigger. On the computer, *King's Quest I–IV* had already launched, but the fifth installment in 1990 replaced the typing interface with point-and-click. And a little game called *Final Fantasy* was released in the United States on the NES.

23. *The Fresh Prince of Bel-Air* **premiered.** And a superstar was launched in Will Smith.

24. With video, was seeing believing? As footage of D.C. mayor Marion Barry smoking crack played a role in his trial, *EW* recalled the fallout from videotapes featuring Patricia Hearst, Rob Lowe, and more.

25. *Jurassic Park* **made its mark in fiction.** "If you're going to do a dinosaur book, people must be munched," author Michael Crichton told *EW*, but "the ideas...are much more important to me than the munches."

The Greats

It isn't an easy job: To find the best, you have to consume a lot of the worst. But naming the finest in movies, TV, music, and books is our never-ending passion. And to then rank the greats of the past 25 years, we've made tough calls: *Friends* vs. *The Sopranos*, Beyoncé vs. Nirvana. Here, our top picks, plus under-the-radar hits, and more.

PULP FICTION

Pulp Fiction
Directed by
Quentin Tarantino (1994)

This low-down dirty tale of L.A. hitmen, palookas, and femmes fatales is a feast of ultraviolent thrills—and also a heady pop-literate consideration of surf rock, foot massages, diner culture, and honor among scoundrels. You'd be hard-pressed by now to name a moment from its time-warping, movie-mad genius that isn't iconic.

SAVING PRIVATE RYAN

2. The *Lord of the Rings* Trilogy
Directed by
Peter Jackson (2001-03)
Peter Jackson did the impossible: He conjured a dark, ravishing vision all his own without desecrating author J.R.R. Tolkien's; he made a nine-hour trilogy that lives and breathes like one movie; he got a riveting performance out of a slithery CG cave dweller with a split personality; and he made fantasy a box office monster.

3. Titanic
Directed by
James Cameron (1997)
The beauty of this epic—the one disaster movie that's also a primal work of popular art— is that it knows all too well the breathless affair between Leonardo DiCaprio and Kate Winslet wouldn't have lasted had it not been for that iceberg. In *Titanic*, it's death that makes love eternal (and worthy of 100 hankies). The sinking of the ship is one of the cinema's great spectacles of beauty and dread.

4. Toy Story
Directed by
John Lasseter (1995)
Yes, it was the first entirely computer-generated feature film, but Pixar's technological achievement paled next to its creative one. Like *Winnie the Pooh* before it, *Toy Story* brought the secret lives of playthings to light with real warmth but also with a ricocheting humor that finally made boring family movies an endangered species.

5. Saving Private Ryan
Directed by
Steven Spielberg (1998)
From the cathartic shock and terror of its opening D-Day sequence, this World War II masterpiece puts us directly inside the consciousness of men in battle and depicts the chaos and slaughter of modern war with a virtuosity no other film has matched. The movie's greatness lies in the way its moral fervor emerges from that blood-spattered bravura.

6. The Silence of the Lambs
Directed by
Jonathan Demme (1991)
A serial-killer film classy enough to win a Best Picture Oscar and gruesome enough to remind you that director Demme once toiled for schlockmeister Roger Corman (who has a cameo). Jodie Foster is lit up with resourcefulness and nerve as an FBI trainee forced to confront every sort of demon. And Anthony Hopkins chills as Hannibal Lecter, a man who knows you should serve white wine with fish and Chianti with census takers.

7. Moulin Rouge!
Directed by
Baz Luhrmann (2001)
Audacious in its madcap use of music, daring in its unabashed embrace of romance, Australian director Baz Luhrmann's *Moulin Rouge* taps into all the passion of the old

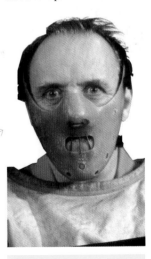

CONTINUES ON PAGE 10 ▶

movie musicals while recharging them for this century.

8 The Matrix
Directed by Andy and Lana Wachowski (1999)
"What is the Matrix?" The answer, as we now know, is that it's the father of two ho-hum sequels. But the Wachowskis' first trip through the virtual-reality looking glass remains an action-movie classic that boasts both bullets and brains.

9 GoodFellas
Directed by Martin Scorsese (1990)
Recall the opening scene: that Pontiac Grand Prix cruising down a highway with something banging in the trunk. Then think of the last shot: Henry Hill (Ray Liotta) marooned on a suburban doorstep in his bathrobe. Now consider all the other classic scenes and set pieces in between. Along with *Taxi Driver* and *Raging*

Bull, this is Scorsese's most ferocious and virtuosic work.

10 Edward Scissorhands
Directed by Tim Burton (1990)
Tim Burton's pastel-colored, break-your-heart career high-point—about a misfit whose clipping skills transform a community—was also the start of many fans' love affair with an elusive, eccentric young man named Johnny Depp.

11 Boogie Nights
Directed by Paul Thomas Anderson (1997)
Boogie Nights is not short on drugs, violence, or sex. But Paul Thomas Anderson's real interest lies in skillfully detailing the pseudo-familial relationships of his porn-industry characters. It's like *The Waltons* but with a massive prosthetic dong.

12 Jerry Maguire
Directed by Cameron Crowe (1996)
Tom Cruise's richest go-for-broke performance. Cameron Crowe's most quotable script. Unbeatable support from Cuba Gooding Jr., Renée Zellweger (in her breakout film), and—remember this little guy?—Jonathan Lipnicki. *Jerry Maguire* is what every big-studio, star-vehicle blockbuster should aspire to be.

13 12 Years a Slave
Directed by Steve McQueen (2013)
This masterpiece is the first

EDWARD SCISSORHANDS

12 YEARS A SLAVE

movie to dramatize the experience of slavery in all its fear and horror. As kidnapped free man Solomon Northup, Chiwetel Ejiofor lets his emotions breathe right through his skin, and Lupita Nyong'o is staggering as a slave girl suffering the torments of the damned. Yet the film balances despair and perseverance, pain and transcendence—and as such, it is a true reckoning with history.

14 The Lion King
Directed by
Rob Minkoff and
Roger Allers (1994)
A gorgeous score from Hans Zimmer, majestic African vistas courtesy of Disney animators, and a plot with *Hamlet*-size ambitions: not bad for a supposed kids' flick.

15 Schindler's List
Directed by
Steven Spielberg (1993)
A shattering tale of unlikely heroism in the face of rank evil. It's easy to forget the considerable risks that Spielberg took in making an extremely long, black-and-white, and essentially starless film about the Holocaust. The movie itself, on the other hand, you will never forget.

CONTINUES ON PAGE 13 ▶

They Won an Oscar for Best Picture, But Did They Make Bank?*

Year	Film	Box Office
1990	Dances With Wolves	$184
1991	The Silence of the Lambs	$130
1992	Unforgiven	$101
1993	Schindler's List	$96
1994	Forrest Gump	$330
1995	Braveheart	$75.6
1996	The English Patient	$78.6
1997	Titanic	$601
1998	Shakespeare in Love	$100
1999	American Beauty	$130
2000	Gladiator	$188
2001	A Beautiful Mind	$171
2002	Chicago	$171
2003	The Lord of the Rings: The Return of the King	$378
2004	Million Dollar Baby	$100
2005	Crash	$54.5
2006	The Departed	$132
2007	No Country for Old Men	$74
2008	Slumdog Millionaire	$141
2009	The Hurt Locker	$17
2010	The King's Speech	$139
2011	The Artist	$44.6
2012	Argo	$136
2013	12 Years a Slave	$56.6
2014	Birdman	$42 (and counting)

*DOMESTIC BOX OFFICE FIGURES IN MILLIONS US

Tom Hanks

HE'S PLAYED MEN AS DIFFERENT AS WALT DISNEY AND ASTRONAUT JIM LOVELL, AND HIS MASTERY OF BOTH COMEDY AND DRAMA HAS EARNED HIM COMPARISONS TO JIMMY STEWART

five  2

OSCAR NOMINATIONS:

(*Big, Philadelphia, Forrest Gump, Saving Private Ryan, Cast Away*)

OSCAR WINS:

(*Philadelphia, Forrest Gump*)

53

seconds his character, Jimmy Dugan, pees in *A League of Their Own*

 26

pounds he lost for *Philadelphia*

 55

pounds he lost for *Cast Away*

1

short stories he's had published in *The New Yorker* (he now has a contract to deliver a collection)

10 MILLION

 Twitter followers

100+

times he's seen *2001: A Space Odyssey*

13

the number of times Wilson's name is spoken in *Cast Away*

 1

number of best-selling apps by him in iTunes (Hanx Writer)

2013

year he made his Broadway debut (in *Lucky Guy*)

1 asteroids named after him (12818 Tomhanks, discovered 4/13/96)

8.5 BILLION

WORLDWIDE GROSS OF HIS MOVIES

12 million

copies of the *Forrest Gump* soundtrack sold

3 MOVIES IN WHICH HE COSTARS WITH MEG RYAN:

Joe Versus the Volcano
1990

Sleepless in Seattle
1993

You've Got Mail
1998

1998

the year he received a square outside Grauman's Chinese Theater

30 days it took him to write the script for *That Thing You Do!*

4

dogs who played Hooch to his Turner

8

times he's hosted *SNL*

10 houses he'd lived in by the time he was 10

square footage of the home in Pacific Palisades he bought in 2010
14,513

$25,000

amount the bench he sat on in *Forrest Gump* sold for at auction in 2013

$50,000

amount he contributed to help pay for Barack Obama's presidential inauguration events

ten

years younger he is than Sally Field, who played his mother in *Forrest Gump*

23

seconds of weightlessness he experienced during each dip of the "Vomit Comet," in which zero-gravity scenes for *Apollo 13* were filmed

---

CONTINUED FROM PAGE 11

16 **Rushmore**
Directed by Wes Anderson (1998)
Wes Anderson's break-through comedy is, like its spiritual predecessor *The Graduate*, a mannered, idio-syncratic, and hilarious coming-of-age tale that makes amazing use of its rock soundtrack and features a decidedly odd love triangle: Bill Murray's middle-aged businessman, Olivia Williams' widowed teacher, and, of course, Jason Schwartzman's ardent schoolboy.

RUSHMORE

CONTINUES ON PAGE 14 ▶

MOVIES CONTINUED FROM PAGE 13

Steven Spielberg originally bought the rights to William Steig's Shrek! in *1991, envisioning it as hand-drawn animation voiced by Bill Murray as Shrek and Steve Martin as Donkey. Better? Worse? We'll never know.*

17 The Dark Knight
Directed by Christopher Nolan (2008)
This magnificently despairing, anarchic film made its first mark with an indelible turn as the Joker by Heath Ledger, who died just months before its release (and was awarded an Oscar posthumously). Viewed again with the passage of time and the changing of the U.S. political landscape, Christopher Nolan's tale of a superhero (Christian Bale) uneasy with his calling in a city anesthetized to matter-of-fact evil takes on new and even more poignant shadings of relevance.

18 Shrek
Directed by Andrew Adamson and Vicky Jenson (2001)
By taking relentless (and funny!) potshots at the Disney formula, the creature with the pea-soup skin and the Mike Myers brogue made ugly the new beautiful. *Shrek* is a feisty but good-natured embrace of the ogre in us all, set to a glorious pop soundtrack.

19 The Social Network
Directed by David Fincher (2010)
With Jesse Eisenberg playing a riveting version of Facebook founder Mark Zuckerberg and Aaron Sorkin spinning the words, director David Fincher created a sharp and enthralling meditation on the intersection of intellectual genius, business ruthlessness, male geekdom, and the sexual insecurities that drive everyone to do everything.

20 The Bourne Supremacy
Directed by Paul Greengrass (2004)
What's more dangerous than an amnesia-stricken government hitman? A vengeance-fueled, amnesia-stricken government hitman. Director Paul Greengrass' sequel made Doug Liman's by-no-means-sluggish original *The Bourne Identity* look like it was stuck in reverse.

21 Brokeback Mountain
Directed by Ang Lee (2005)
The cool move here would be to ignore the fact that Heath Ledger and Jake Gyllenhaal enacted a truly groundbreaking love story—and simply concentrate on what a gorgeous, nuanced, heartbreaking movie *Brokeback* is for people of any sexual orientation. But Ang Lee's undeniably romantic movie did break ground. It reached, and moved, mainstream audiences in ways that no gay movie ever had before.

22 Fargo
Directed by Joel and Ethan Coen (1996)
The Coen brothers have always been great yarn spinners, and *Fargo* is their trickiest, funniest, most perfectly told tale. Everything that goes wrong in its desperate kidnap-ransom scheme does so in a landscape so muffled by snow and Scandinavian-bred, low-affect courtesy that even murderous passion comes out goofy. Warming *Fargo*'s core is Frances McDormand as the pregnant chief of police, who balances investigating a triple homicide with stopping to pick up fishing worms for her husband on her way home.

23 Fight Club
Directed by David Fincher (1999)
This violent, hilarious, and tricksy dissection of modern manhood represents a career pinnacle for director David Fincher, Brad Pitt, Edward Norton, and Meat Loaf. Yes, it's even better than *Bat Out of Hell*.

24 The Hurt Locker
Directed by Kathryn Bigelow (2008)
What makes this extraordinary Iraq battlefield drama so

essential is its pinpoint accuracy in mapping the disorienting roads a man—an Army bomb-disposal specialist played by Jeremy Renner—can walk down when his job keeps him so close to death, working for what sometimes feels like a distant principle. Both the movie and director Kathryn Bigelow won well-deserved Oscars—with Bigelow breaking ground to become the only female director to do so.

25 Guardians of the Galaxy

Directed by James Gunn (2014) Marvel's band of intergalactic antiheroes goosed anarchic life into a genre that tends to get mired in existential heaviness. What's not to love about a squabbling posse of misfits that includes Chris Pratt's cocky Star-Lord, Zoe Saldana's green-skinned assassin, a foul-mouthed raccoon, and a grunting tree named Groot? ∎

FIGHT CLUB

Bonus!

Best Heist Films

Ocean's Eleven	2001
Inside Man	2006
The Italian Job	2003
Heat	1995
Three Kings	1999

Most Creepy Horror Films

The Orphanage	2007
The Ring	2002
The Blair Witch Project	1999
The Others	2001
The Conjuring	2013

Great Summer Blockbusters

Independence Day	1996
Terminator 2: Judgment Day	199)
Jurassic Park	1993
The Dark Knight	2008
Forrest Gump	1994

Best Buddy Comedies

White Men Can't Jump	1992
The Hangover	2009
Superbad	2007
Hot Fuzz	2007
The Heat	2013

Memorable Movie Catchphrases

Jack Nicholson

"You can't handle the truth!" *A Few Good Men* 1992

"Hasta la vista, baby." *Terminator 2* 1991

"The first rule of Fight Club is: You do not talk about Fight Club." *Fight Club* 1999

"You had me at hello." *Jerry Maguire* 1996

"I see dead people." *The Sixth Sense* 1999

Comedies

OFFICE SPACE

1 The Big Lebowski

Directed by Joel and Ethan Coen (1998)
This masterpiece of anti-story-telling boasts Jeff Bridges' most defining role—a hilariously passive, drug-addled amateur sleuth (imagine Tommy Chong as Philip Marlowe in *The Big Sleep*). As his pal Walter Sobchak, a super-articulate Vietnam vet, John Goodman is the film's irresistible force to the Dude's eminently movable object. CLASSIC LINE: *"That rug really tied the room together."*

2 Office Space

Directed by Mike Judge (1999)
A box office dud on its release, Mike Judge's satire of workplace drudgery went on to become sacred to all those who've ever come down with a case of the Mondays. Twentieth Century Fox not only struggled to market the dark comedy but also didn't really get it themselves. But after *Office Space* was released on DVD in 2000, a fan base began to build, and eventually the movie that had grossed only $10.8 million became a cult phenomenon. CLASSIC LINE: *"I did absolutely nothing, and it was everything that I thought it could be."*

3 South Park: Bigger, Longer & Uncut

Directed by Trey Parker (1999)
With jokes about abortion, incest, and Saddam Hussein, this is one of the most offensive—and most uproarious—movies ever made. The plot (the boys sneak into a deliriously scatological movie and emerge with a vocabulary so obscene it sends the town into an uproar) rollicks ahead with few dead spots, and the musical numbers brilliantly parody/honor the conventions of Broadway show tunes and Disney-formula ditties. WHAT WE SAID THEN: The funniest, most risk-taking, most incisive movie of the summer. A-

4 There's Something About Mary

Directed by Bobby and Peter Farrelly (1998)

When people staggered out of theaters the year this movie raked in more than $176 million, they talked about cans of whup-ass and painful zipper incidents and unfortunate lap dogs. But first and foremost, they raved about the hair-gel scene.

CLASSIC LINE: *"Some of my best friends didn't know my name."*

5 Dazed and Confused

Directed by Richard Linklater (1993)

This free-flowing pic about the last day (and night) of high school in 1976 doesn't just capture the clothes, the slang, the cars, the vintage rock songs; it gets the attitude of carefree dilapidation, the ramshackle, good-time delirium, that marked a generation of happy

CONTINUES ON PAGE 18 ▶

POP CULTURE OBSESSION

Biopics

FASCINATING LIVES, FROM WILLIAM WALLACE TO SISTER HELEN PREJEAN

1	BRAVEHEART	7	RAY	13	CAPOTE	18	THE LAST KING OF	22	BASQUIAT

1 **BRAVEHEART**
William Wallace, 13th-century Scottish warrior

2 **ELIZABETH**
Elizabeth I of England

3 **LINCOLN**
16th President Abraham Lincoln

4 **LA VIE EN ROSE**
French singer Édith Piaf

5 **SCHINDLER'S LIST**
German Oskar Schindler

6 **THE AVIATOR**
Inventor Howard Hughes

7 **RAY**
Singer Ray Charles

8 **ED WOOD**
Director "Ed" Wood Jr.

9 **THE NOTORIOUS BETTIE PAGE**
Pinup model Bettie Page

10 **A BEAUTIFUL MIND**
Nobel Laureate of Economics John Nash

11 **MALCOLM X**
Revolutionary Malcolm X

12 **WALK THE LINE**
Country singer Johnny Cash

13 **CAPOTE**
Writer Truman Capote

14 **NIXON**
37th President Richard Nixon

15 **ALI**
Professional boxer Muhammad Ali

16 **WHAT'S LOVE GOT TO DO WITH IT?**
Singer Tina Turner

17 **BEFORE NIGHT FALLS**
Cuban poet and novelist Reinaldo Arenas

18 **THE LAST KING OF SCOTLAND**
Ugandan dictator and self-styled "King" Idi Amin

19 **MILK**
Gay rights activist and politician Harvey Milk

20 **AMERICAN SPLENDOR**
Comic-book creator and writer Harvey Pekar

21 **PRIVATE PARTS**
Shock jock and radio star Howard Stern

22 **BASQUIAT**
Street artist Jean-Michel Basquiat

23 **DEAD MAN WALKING**
Sister Helen Prejean and death row prisoner Matthew Poncelet

24 **THE DIVING BELL AND THE BUTTERFLY**
Stroke survivor Jean-Dominique Bauby

25 **THE SOCIAL NETWORK**
Facebook founder Mark Zuckerberg

COMEDIES CONTINUED FROM PAGE 17

THE 40-YEAR-OLD VIRGIN

stoner burnouts. Richard Linklater is no mere pop anthropologist—he's an inspired entertainer whose characters are subtle, offbeat, moving, and bracingly life-size, and as he captures the comic goofiness of the time, he also evokes its liberating spirit. WHAT WE SAID THEN: Maybe the most slyly funny and dead-on portrait of American teenage life ever made. **A**

6 Groundhog Day

Directed by Harold Ramis (1993)
What strikes you now isn't how simultaneously barbed and warm Bill Murray is as he lives Feb. 2 over and over, but how simultaneously bleak and hopeful this modern classic feels: Every day is cold and lonely, the film insists, yet we can still make the most of it. CLASSIC LINE: *"This is one time where television really fails to capture the true excitement of a large squirrel predicting the weather."*

7 The 40-Year-Old Virgin

Directed by Judd Apatow (2005)
In his breakout performance, Steve Carell sacrifices his dignity—and chest hair—to play a meek, action-figure-collect-

CONTINUES ON PAGE 21 ▶

Our Favorite Foreign Films

MEXICO
1. *Amores Perros*
2. *Y Tu Mamá También*

BRAZIL
3. *City of God*
4. *Central Station*

DENMARK
5. *The Celebration*

FRANCE
6. *Amour*
7. *Amélie*

SPAIN
8. *All About My Mother*
9. *Pan's Labyrinth*

ITALY
10. *Life Is Beautiful*
11. *Il Postino*

GERMANY
12. *The Lives of Others*
13. *Run Lola Run*

CZECH REPUBLIC
14. *Kolya*

POLAND
15. *Ida*

IRAN
17. *A Separation*

RUSSIA
16. *Leviathan*

JAPAN
18. *Spirited Away*

SOUTH KOREA
19. *Oldboy*

TAIWAN
20. *Eat Drink Man Woman*

CHINA
21. *Infernal Affairs*
22. *Farewell My Concubine*
23. *Raise the Red Lantern*
24. *Crouching Tiger, Hidden Dragon*

SOUTH AFRICA
25. *Tsotsi*

Bill Murray

HIS RASCALLY CHARM AND DEADPAN HUMOR HAVE DELIGHTED FANS FOR DECADES — SO HE'S GOT THAT GOING FOR HIM

6 movies he made with Harold Ramis

7 movies he's made with Wes Anderson

4 years he dropped out of acting after *Ghostbusters* to study philosophy in France, among other things

7 GOLF HANDICAP HE GOT DOWN TO (MORE RECENTLY HE'S SAID HE'S BETWEEN A 7 AND AN 11)

2011 YEAR HE AND D.A. POINTS WON THE AT&T PEBBLE BEACH NATIONAL PRO-AM GOLF TOURNAMENT

one book he's co-written: *Cinderella Story*, a golf-related memoir

3 days *Meatballs*, his first starring role, had already been shooting before he agreed to show up

15 miles he rode a bike every day from the set of 2014's *St. Vincent* to where he was staying in Williamsburg, Brooklyn

40+ appearances on various David Letterman talk shows

1 episode of *Seinfeld* he's said he watched (the finale; he didn't like it)

1-800 phone number he uses instead of an agent

$1 amount he's said he spent on Christmas presents one year for his cash-strapped family as a kid — "getting everybody something that cost a dime."

nine
children in his Irish Catholic family growing up—six boys and three girls

six
children he has (all sons, with two wives)

17
age he was when his father, who suffered from diabetes, passed away

times he was bitten by the groundhog in *Groundhog Day*

2

8,000+
square footage of dining space in Murray Bros. Caddyshack, a restaurant in St. Augustine, Fla., Bill and his five brothers own

50
age at which, he said when he was 30, he didn't "want to be doing movies" anymore

}65
age he is now

ONE MOVIE HE'S CODIRECTED (*QUICK CHANGE*, 1990)

10
pounds of marijuana found in his luggage at O'Hare Airport on his 20th birthday; he pled guilty and was sentenced to five years probation

one
Oscar nomination
(*Lost in Translation*)

twelve
months it took Sofia Coppola to persuade him to do *Lost in Translation*

characters he's played who jauntily brandish a cigarette holder (Hunter S. Thompson in *Where the Buffalo Roam*; FDR in *Hyde Park on Hudson*)

70
SNL episodes he was on between 1997 and 1980

CONTINUED FROM PAGE 18

ing doofus who's never had sex; Catherine Keener is the woman of his undeflowered dreams. This smart, sweet-but-raunchy comedy proved to be a blissfully refreshing alternative to typical studio summer fare. **WHAT WE SAID THEN:** Buoyantly clever and amusing, a comedy of horny embarrassment that has the inspiration to present a middle-aged virgin's dilemma as a projection of all our romantic anxieties. **A-**

8 Waiting for Guffman
Directed by Christopher Guest (1996)
This madcap gem of a mock-umentary follows the hapless residents of Blaine, Mo., as they attempt to put on a musical for the town's sesquicentennial. Guest plays their morosely flamboyant leader, Corky St. Clair, like he's Ed Wood in the body of Harvey Fierstein,

and while the Blaine thespians are shamelessly talentless, the beauty of the film is that they're never just ridiculous. **CLASSIC LINE:** *"It's like a Hitchcock movie, you know, where you're thrown into a rubber bag and put in the trunk of a car. You find people."*

9 Wedding Crashers
Directed by David Dobkin (2005)
The neo-retro-hetero duo of Vince Vaughn and Owen Wilson shine as champion skirt-chasers who wangle their way into strangers' weddings, the better to pick up chicks susceptible to the romance in the air and the champagne in their glasses. The two meet their matches, as they must— every horndog has his day—in an unabashedly jiggly, bawdy, it's-all-good comedy. **CLASSIC LINE:** *"I've got a stage five clinger!"*

CONTINUES ON PAGE 22 ▶

COMEDIES CONTINUED FROM PAGE 21

ELECTION

10 Superbad

Directed by
Greg Mottola (2007)
The world got that McLovin feelin' from this libidinous, hilarious tale about male high schoolers trying to get laid via booze. It revolves around two biological organs—and thankfully, it's the film's heart that ultimately prevails. CLASSIC LINE: *"McLovin? What kind of a stupid name is that, Fogell? What, are you trying to be an Irish R&B singer?"*

11 Tropic Thunder

Directed by
Ben Stiller (2008)
A spot-on skewering of Hollywood about a cast of actors off on an acting adventure on the set of a war picture in Southeast Asia. Filled with terrific grotesques—from Robert Downey Jr.'s never-breaks-character thesp to Tom Cruise's mercenary studio chief—it's also a smart and agile dissection of art, fame, and the chutzpah of big-budget productions. WHAT WE SAID THEN: This is Stiller's Hellzapoppin' *Apocalypse Now*—the ultimate fighting machine of comedies about the making of movies. A

12 Election

Directed by
Alexander Payne (1999)
As win-at-all-costs high school presidential candidate Tracy Flick, Reese Witherspoon introduced a new archetype for craven ambition. Director Alexander Payne doesn't go easy on anybody. CLASSIC LINE: *"It's like my mom says, 'The weak are always trying to sabotage the strong.'"*

13 The Grand Budapest Hotel

Directed by
Wes Anderson (2014)
A looser, freer invention than most Wes Anderson films, *The Grand Budapest Hotel*—starring Ralph Fiennes as a hotel con-

Under-the-Radar Movies Worth Seeking Out

24 HOUR PARTY PEOPLE 2002 | BACKBEAT 1994 | BAMBOOZLED 2000 | BOX OF MOON LIGHT 1996 | BUBBA HO-TEP 2002 | CHUCK & BUCK 2000 | COLD COMFORT FARM 1995 | THE DAYTRIPPERS 1996 | ENTER THE VOID 2009 | EVE'S BAYOU 1997 | FISH TANK 2009 | FLY AWAY HOME 1996 | GHOST DOG: THE WAY OF THE SAMURAI 1999 | HACHI: A DOG'S TALE 2009 | HAPPY ACCIDENTS 2000 | IDIOCRACY 2006 | THE IRON GIANT 1999 | I'VE LOVED YOU SO LONG 2008 | LOVE & BASKETBALL 2000 | THE MAGDALENE SISTERS 2002 | MEMORIES OF MURDER 2003 | MOON 2009 | NEXT STOP WONDERLAND 1998 | THE ORPHANAGE 2007 | WALKING AND TALKING 1996

cierge who romances elderly patrons in a fictional European nation near the start of World War II—is a marvelous contraption, a wheels-within-wheels thriller that's pure oxygenated movie play. CLASSIC LINE: *"I don't know what sort of cream they've put on you down at the morgue, but I want some."*

14 Napoleon Dynamite

Directed by Jared Hess (2004) Only freakin' idiots could fail to chuckle at this tale of a high school misfit in a tiny Idaho town whose skills include shooting wolverines, drawing ligers, and breaking out some awesome dance moves. Fox Searchlight snapped this $400,000 oddball up at Sundance and turned it into a sleeper hit that grossed $45 million. CLASSIC LINE: *"Sure, the worldwide web is great, but you, you make me 'salivate.'"*

15 Old School

Directed by Todd Phillips (2003) Three grown men (Will

NAPOLEON DYNAMITE

Ferrell, Vince Vaughn, and Luke Wilson) decide to roll back the clock to a time when burping, bonging, and banging were de rigueur: They start a new college fraternity. CLASSIC LINE: *"I wasn't looking for a girl like that." "Well, Columbus wasn't looking for America, my man, but that turned out to be pretty okay for everyone."*

16 Shaun of the Dead

Directed by Edgar Wright (2004) The daffy, innately British joke that propels this cheeky comedy is that although zombies have risen up in a nondescript outpost of London, slacker wankers Shaun (Simon Pegg)

and his best pal and roommate, Ed (Nick Frost), are too slack, wankerish, and blitheringly British to notice. CLASSIC LINE: *"I don't think I've got it in me to shoot my flatmate, my mum, and my girlfriend all in the same evening."*

17 Juno

Directed by Jason Reitman (2007) Though it's about a high schooler who gets pregnant and chooses to give the baby up for adoption, this blithe charmer of a movie forgoes political debate about right to life/right to choose/right to make jokes about teenage sex to focus solely on what it's like to be the title character, Juno. Played by the radiantly no-nonsense Ellen Page (who earned an Oscar nod), she's what every whip-smart young woman inspired by *My So-Called Life, Freaks and Geeks,* and *Daria* should be. Minus the unprotected sex. CLASSIC LINE: *"Yeah, I'm a legend. You know, they call me the cautionary whale."*

CONTINUES ON PAGE 25 ▶

Movies
That Score

- **RUDY** Sean Astin dreams of Notre Dame football in the ultimate underdog story. Grown men will cry.

- **REMEMBER THE TITANS** Denzel Washington leads a desegregated football team into the post-Civil Rights '70s. A moving weepie with a tough heart.

- **THE BLIND SIDE** A wrong-side-of-the-tracks football prodigy meets the tough, blonde, no-bull mentor of our dreams. Of course Bullock won the Oscar.

- **WE ARE MARSHALL** An extreme vision of the healing power of sports: After a devastating plane crash, a new coach leads a grieving community to victory.

- **FRIDAY NIGHT LIGHTS** A dreamy, panoramic examination of a year in the life of small-town football. The TV show's pretty good, too.

- **MONEYBALL** The baseball movie for the Nerd Age, with Brad Pitt using advanced math to transform underdogs into a powerhouse team.

- **A LEAGUE OF THEIR OWN** The great American sports movie about everyone who isn't a man, with an all-star team (Madonna! Rosie!) and a tense sibling-rivalry showdown.

- **THE ROOKIE** A never-better Dennis Quaid plays an Everyguy high school teacher taking a last shot at the pros.

- **42** In the first Jackie Robinson biopic, the athlete played himself. Six decades later, Chadwick Boseman brings the boundary-breaking ballplayer back to life.

- **GLORY ROAD** When Texas Western College integrates its basketball team, the toughest battles happen off the court. An inspiring look at how athletics became Civil Rights' front lines.

- **COACH CARTER** A high school sports movie about the importance of good grades. Samuel L. Jackson is the coach with more on his mind than the game.

- **THE FIGHTER** The title should be plural, since every

42

COOL RUNNINGS

MILLION DOLLAR BABY

RUDY

one onscreen is locked in combat. Brother vs. brother, mother vs. son, family vs. family, and family vs. everyone else.

- **ALI** Less a biopic than an expansive look at how a wild period in history made a brilliant man—and how that brilliant man made history.

- **MILLION DOLLAR BABY** You can smell the sweat and tears in Clint Eastwood's pugilist melodrama.

- **CINDERELLA MAN** It's the Great Depression, and America needs a comeback. Thank goodness for Russell Crowe, a little guy climbing to boxing's big leagues.

- **BEND IT LIKE BECKHAM** Feminism? The immigrant experience? Heavy stuff. But this Big Idea, high-energy British film is light on its feet.

- **INVICTUS** When Nelson Mandela asks a sports superstar to save the country by winning a championship, it's cosmic stakes.

- **THE DAMNED UNITED** As played by Michael Sheen, almost-legendary British football manager Brian Clough is a brilliant, spiteful, self-defeating egomaniac: British football's Walter White.

- **TIN CUP** Kevin Costner's made plenty of baseball movies, but he's at his most charming as the slacker golf guru in this low-key romcom.

- **THE WRESTLER** In which Mickey Rourke plays Mickey Rourke, more or less: a god in ruins brought down to devastating human size.

- **MIRACLE** Watch out, commies! The Cold War freezes over at the 1980 Winter Olympics. Kurt Russell is the tough coach leading his boys to victory.

- **COOL RUNNINGS** Jamaican Bobsled Team: That phrase alone is a triumph of the human spirit.

- **LORDS OF DOGTOWN** A bunch of hippie surfers reinvent skateboarding. It's like watching the 1970s invent the 1990s one trick at a time.

- **SEABISCUIT** Small, wobbly-kneed, unimpressive until he starts impressing: The titular horse is a palpable metaphor for everyone struggling against their own limitations.

- **DODGEBALL** And now for something completely different: a hilarious satire of sports-movie cliché that's also a thrilling team-of-misfits triumph in its own right.

18 The Hangover
Directed by
Todd Phillips (2009)

Going to Las Vegas for a "wild" bachelor party is now the ultimate hedonist cliché, and the fun of *The Hangover* is that the film completely understands this. Its four main characters aren't daring or cool; they're an unglamorous Everyguy quartet, and when they wake up in their trashed villa with a tiger in the bathroom, a baby in the cabinet, and a missing tooth as well as a missing groom, the discovery of what happened becomes the perfect comeuppance to their tidy fantasy of Vegas bliss. **WHAT WE SAID THEN:** *The Hangover* is a riff on what the stuff you do when you're really out of control says about you. **B**

19 Best in Show
Directed by
Christopher Guest (2000)

This dogumentary barks up big laughs with a blue-ribbon comedy ensemble that includes Parker Posey, Jennifer Coolidge, Eugene Levy, Catherine O'Hara, and a pre-

Glee Jane Lynch. The animal actors perfectly mirror their human counterparts, but the heavily improvised, wonderfully ridiculous dialogue provides the movie's most satisfying bite. **CLASSIC LINE:** *"And to think that in some countries these dogs are eaten."*

20 Clueless
Directed by
Amy Heckerling (1995)

A few references in this high school comedy—very loosely based on Jane

Austen's *Emma*—may have today's teens reaching for their history books. But writer-director Amy Heckerling's script still crackles, while Alicia Silverstone's central performance as a lovable airhead remains, like, totally awesome. **CLASSIC LINE:** *"Do you prefer 'fashion victim' or 'ensembly challenged'?"*

21 Bridesmaids
Directed by
Paul Feig (2011)

A comedy about the complicated friendships between women that's so beguiling and heartrending that even its gross-out humor (that explosive scene where food poisoning takes hold in a bridal boutique) is rooted in real, recognizable emotions. *Bridesmaids* leaves every cookie-cutter "chick flick" miles behind. **CLASSIC LINE:** *"You are like the maid of dishonor."*

22 Zoolander
Directed by
Ben Stiller (2001)

Ben Stiller's Blue Steel-y satire about air-headed male supermodels was a welcome blast of comedy when it was released two weeks after 9/11. Since then it's become such a cult favorite that the announcement of a sequel set for 2016 (made by Stiller and Owen Wilson in character on the runway at Paris Fashion Week, of course) made international headlines. **CLASSIC**

CONTINUES ON PAGE 26 ▶

LINE: *"Moisture is the essence of wetness, and wetness is the essence of beauty."*

23 Austin Powers: International Man of Mystery

Directed by Jay Roach (1997) Before the shameless sequels, the original Bond spoof rocks. With his horn-rims and dirty crooked teeth, his crushed-velvet jackets and horrifying psychedelic flares, Mike Myers as Austin—cryogenically frozen in the '60s and thawed out in the present day—is the geekiest swinger who ever lived, so square he's almost hip. And in the dual role of hilariously arch supervillain Dr. Evil, he's worth every bit of that 1 million dollar ransom. CLASSIC LINE: *"I'm going to place him in an easily escapable situation involving an overly elaborate and exotic death."*

24 The Birdcage

Directed by Mike Nichols (1996) In the hands of director Mike Nichols and writer Elaine May, *The Birdcage* is an enchantingly witty and humane entertainment about a gay couple (Robin Williams and Nathan Lane) thrown into a tizzy when they must host a dinner for their son, his fiancée, and her rabidly right-wing senator father (Gene Hackman) and mother. The more they try to pretend to be something they're not, the more obvious it is who they really are, and the punchlines are as deliciously irrepressible as the characters. CLASSIC LINE: *"Shouldn't you be holding the crucifix? It is THE prop for martyrs!"*

25 Clerks

Directed by Kevin Smith (1994) With its cruddy lensing and sound, its atmosphere of zonked deadpan boredom, and its characters whose defining trait is their complete indifference to everything around them, Smith's way-low-budget debut feels like a bootleg copy of an adolescent mind. CLASSIC LINE: *"This job would be great if it wasn't for the fucking customers."* ∎

Take a Seat, See the World

NORTH AMERICA

1. **BOTTLE SHOCK**
   (Napa Valley, Calif.)
2. **500 DAYS OF SUMMER**
   (LA)
3. **THE TREE OF LIFE**
   (Texas)
4. **BEGIN AGAIN** (NYC)
5. **FRIDA** (Mexico)

SOUTH PACIFIC

6. **THE DESCENDANTS**
   (Hawaii)

SOUTH AMERICA

7. **THE MOTORCYCLE DIARIES** (South America: Patagonia, Chile, Peru, Amazon River)

ARCTIC

8. **THE SECRET LIFE OF WALTER MITTY** (Iceland)

ASIA

22. **LOST IN TRANSLATION** (Tokyo)

23. **CHUNGKING EXPRESS** (Hong Kong)

SOUTHEAST ASIA

24. **THE BEACH** (various locations in Thailand including Krabi and Phi Phi Leh Island, near Phuket)

EUROPE

9. **THE SECRET OF ROAN INISH** (Donegal, Ireland)

10. **NOTTING HILL** (London)

11. **IN BRUGES** (Belgium)

12. **MIDNIGHT IN PARIS** (Paris)

13. **AMÉLIE** (Paris)

14. **VICKY CRISTINA BARCELONA** (Barcelona, Spain)

15. **THE WAY** (the Camino de Santiago, northwestern Spain)

16. **UNDER THE TUSCAN SUN** (Cortona, Italy)

17. **THE TALENTED MR. RIPLEY** (Rome and Venice)

18. **BEFORE MIDNIGHT** (Southern Peloponnese, Greece)

SOUTH ASIA

19. **THE BEST EXOTIC MARIGOLD HOTEL** (Rajasthan, India)

AFRICA

20. **THE SHELTERING SKY** (Morocco)

21. **THE CONSTANT GARDENER** (Lake Turkana, Kenya)

AUSTRALIA

25. **ADVENTURES OF PRISCILLA, QUEEN OF THE DESERT** (Australia)

Television

TV'S BEST TAKE US INSIDE THE OVAL OFFICE, A METH LAB, AND SOME VERY DYSFUNCTIONAL LIVING ROOMS

THE SIMPSONS

1 The Simpsons
Fox (1989–present)

It will go down as the most revered, beloved comedy in TV history. For 26 seasons, this exquisitely crafted gag machine has been rat-a-tatting out penetrating deconstructions and celebrations of the dysfunctional American clan. Name another show that has created as rich and dense a universe as Springfield: Those hundreds of little yellow characters feel real (even "I love to get blotto" Otto), and we all hail Simpson patriarch Homer because his joy is as palpable as his stupidity is stunning. Bottom line: We *d'oh!*n't know what anyone would do without *The Simpsons*.

2 The Sopranos
HBO (1999–2007)

To call it a Mafia drama misses the point; it's the quintessential family drama. *The Sopranos* infuses themes of love and betrayal with foreboding subtext and jet-black humor. And it gave rise to TV's supreme antihero, Tony Soprano, played by the inimitable James Gandolfini.

3 Seinfeld
NBC (1989–98)

The most cunning, self-absorbed, neurotic, minutiae-obsessed sitcom ever—yada yada yada.

4 The X-Files
Fox (1993–2002)

The chemistry between David Duchovny and Gillian Anderson is out of this world, the spooky visuals unmatched. We still have no idea what's up with the truth—still out there, is it?—and creator Chris Carter, who understands this, will bring back the stars to investigate further in a 2016

THE X-FILES

series. (For more on this paranormal gem see: pages 36-43.)

5 **Sex and the City**
HBO (1998-2004)

On the surface, it's a saucy peek at the sexploits of four single NYC women seeking long-term relationships or at least a good one-nighter. Though it went to many unexpected places to mine its money moments (see: funky spunk), it resonated because of its unflinching honesty. Women saw themselves right on the screen. (In case you're wondering, we're a Miranda.)

6 **Breaking Bad**
AMC (2008-2013)

Over five seasons, creator Vince Gilligan cranked up the tension and the moral ambiguity on his meth-making drama, taking Walter White from mild-mannered chemistry prof to drug kingpin who finally admitted, as he sought to right some of his wrongs, "I liked it. I was good at it. And I was really—I was alive." With enthralling performances by Aaron Paul, Anna Gunn, and especially Bryan Cranston,

CONTINUES ON PAGE 30 ▶

Bonus!

Underrated TV Series
Rectify

Enlightened

Strike Back

Joan of Arcadia

Southland

Creepiest Series
American Horror Story: Asylum

Twin Peaks

Hannibal

The X-Files

The Following

Best TV Movies
Doing Time on Maple Drive

And the Band Played On

Miss Rose White

Recount

Introducing Dorothy Dandridge

Live From Baghdad

Bury My Heart at Wounded Knee

Grey Gardens

Temple Grandin

The Normal Heart

Memorable TV Catchphrases:

"D'oh!!" *The Simpsons*

"A George divided against itself cannot stand." *Seinfeld*

"How *you* doin'?" *Friends*

"It's gonna be legen–wait for it–dary." *How I Met Your Mother*

"Let's hug it out, bitch!" *Entourage*

Jason Alexander

Jeremy Piven

this was masterful neo-noir.

7 Lost
ABC (2004-2010)

This exotic survival saga about redemption and community started earthy and existential and finished esoteric and mystic, sparking endless discussion and frustrating some of its fans in the process. What is inarguable is that its tantalizing, labyrinthine mysteries helped change the way we watch and talk about television. (We dissect *Lost* further in Cult TV.)

8 Friends
NBC (1994-2004)

Snappy writing. Snappier haircuts. Could we *be* more succinct?

9 The Wire
HBO (2002-08)

David Simon's unflinching take on Baltimore is epic in scope and journalistic in detail, using a police wiretap as a metaphor for the dizzyingly complex web that connects the drug-infested streets to the police, schools, and politicians. Pluck one

THE OFFICE

strand and watch the spiders and flies skitter into action.

10 South Park
Comedy Central (1997-present)

Those are some mighty nice lives you got there, celebrities. It'd be a damn shame if some construction-paper third-graders from Nowheresville came along and witheringly mocked your limited talent, shallow

understanding of geopolitical conflicts, and questionable sexuality. Yep, damn shame.

11 The Good Wife
CBS (2009-present)

A courtroom drama, a family saga, even a thriller, *The Good Wife* is the flourless chocolate cake of TV: rich and dense. It's a show that takes chances—witness the love affair between Alicia (Julianna Margulies) and

Will (Josh Charles), followed by one of the most shocking deaths in non-cable history.

12 The Daily Show
Comedy Central (1996-present)

Psst! All you nightly network news anchors—were you looking for your trenchant journalistic skepticism? 'Cause we found it . . . on a comedy channel. With Jon Stewart leaving—taking boatloads of Emmy awards with him— it remains to be seen what the show morphs into, but in the hands of Stewart (who took over in 1999), his writers, and his correspondents, it became a satirical powerhouse and a primary source of news for millions.

13 Buffy the Vampire Slayer
The WB (1997-2001); UPN (2001-03)
Few would have guessed that a toothless, one-joke movie would inspire such a brilliant, layered series. By turns scary, romantic, funny, and heart-breaking, *Buffy* proves that a show about teens need not alienate older viewers. (For more see: pages 36-43.)

14 Mad Men
AMC (2007-2015)
Like ad exec Don Draper himself, this series had its ups and downs. But its portrait of 1960s-era office and sexual politics was finely honed and mesmerizing, and the questions sur-

rounding the kind of man Don would ultimately become were always, thanks to Jon Hamm's first-rate portrayal, rich and potent. Finally, it may be the *Mad* women who surprised us most: Betty's suburban ennui, Joan's ambitious awakening, Peggy's trailblazing talents.

15 The Office (U.K. version)
BBC Two (2001-03)
Co-creators Ricky Gervais and Stephen Merchant taught us that funny is when a thankless, dead-end, penny-ante joke of a job at a sullen workplace headed by a deluded, boorish, pompous ass of a boss happens to someone else.

16 ER
NBC (1994-2009)
For 15 powerful seasons, from the budding superstardom of George Clooney to Maura Tierney's weekly acting seminars, this medical juggernaut elevated ensemble work, appropriately, to a science.

CONTINUES ON PAGE 32 ▶

Lauded by the Critics, But Did the Emmys Agree?

1990-2010	*Law & Order*	2
1990-1991	*Twin Peaks*	0
1993-1999	*Homicide: Life on the Street*	3
1993-2005	*NYPD Blue*	16
1994-2009	*ER*	7
1994-1995	*My So-Called Life*	0
1997-2003	*Buffy the Vampire Slayer*	0
1997-2003	*Oz*	0
1999-2008	*The Sopranos*	18
1999-2006	*The West Wing*	17
2001-2005	*Six Feet Under*	3
2001-2010	*24*	5
2002-2008	*The Shield*	1
2002-2008	*The Wire*	0
2004-2010	*Lost*	4
2004-2012	*House M.D.*	2
2006-2011	*Friday Night Lights*	2
2007-2015	*Mad Men*	7
2008-2013	*Breaking Bad*	12
2009-PRESENT	*The Good Wife*	5
2010-PRESENT	*Sherlock*	3
2011-PRESENT	*Homeland*	6
2013-PRESENT	*House of Cards*	1
2013-PRESENT	*Masters of Sex*	1
2013-PRESENT	*The Americans*	0

*EMMYS WON AS OF 2014, FOR SERIES, WRITING, ACTING, AND DIRECTING

17 Beverly Hills, 90210
Fox (1990-2000)

Those five digits are much more than a zip code. They created a sexy new template for teen drama, caused significant underage squealing (OMG, Jason Priestley! Luke Perry!), and spun off four sequels or remakes, helping build the Fox brand.

18 Game of Thrones
HBO (2011-present)

Fantasy never felt so real. HBO's epic adaptation of George R.R. Martin's *A Song of Ice and Fire* novels revels in hero-decapitating, wedding-massacring, dragon-swooping suspense, and yet it features a large cast of characters whose schemes and dilemmas viewers care about.

19 Roseanne
ABC (1988-97)

Before all those comedian-fronted sitcoms became studies in marital hostility, Roseanne Barr and TV hubby John Goodman showed us the frustrations and small, loving victories of a real middle-class American family. Okay, a real family that gets surreal in its last season, but still.

20 The West Wing
NBC (1999-2006)

The Bartlet administration began during a time of great prosperity for our dear country; it wasn't until things went south that this show's true value as escapist political porn became apparent. Yes, Virginia, idealism and government can mix . . . on TV, at least.

21 Gilmore Girls
The WB (2000-06); The CW (2006-07)

Never has there been a more enviable mother-child bond than the one between Lorelai (Lauren Graham) and Rory Gilmore (Alexis Bledel). Creator Amy Sherman-Palladino, mistress of witty banter, should script everyone's adolescence.

22 Chappelle's Show
Comedy Central (2003-06)

Okay, Dave, our stomachs have finally stopped hurting from laughing so hard. You can come back now. Dave?

CHAPPELLE'S SHOW

BEVERLY HILLS, 90210

Big Laughs Landed Emmys (Or Not)

1988–1997	*Roseanne*	4
1988–1998	*Murphy Brown*	15
1989–1998	*Seinfeld*	7
1990–1995	*Northern Exposure*	3
1990–1996	*The Fresh Prince of Bel-Air*	0 →
1992–1998	*The Larry Sanders Show*	3
1992–1999	*Mad About You*	10
2003–2006; 2013–PRESENT	*Arrested Development*	4
1993–2004	*Frasier*	25
1994–2004	*Friends*	6
1997–2002	*Ally McBeal*	3
1998–2004	*Sex and the City*	4
1998–2006	*Will & Grace*	9
1999–2000	*Freaks and Geeks*	0
1999–PRESENT	*Curb Your Enthusiasm*	1
2005–2013	*The Office*	3
2005–2014	*How I Met Your Mother*	0
2006–2011	*30 Rock*	11
2007–PRESENT	*The Big Bang Theory*	5
2009–2015	*Parks and Recreation*	0
2009–PRESENT	*Modern Family*	17
2009–PRESENT	*Community*	0
2010–PRESENT	*Louie*	3
2012–PRESENT	*Girls*	0
2012–PRESENT	*Veep*	4

*EMMYS WON AS OF 2014, FOR SERIES, WRITING, ACTING, AND DIRECTING

23 **Law & Order**
NBC (1990–2010)
"Doink-doink?" "Chung-chung?" The debate still rages on how to spell that sound. But no one is arguing over whether a show can divide itself into discrete halves with their own set of characters, survive cast revolutions, rip from the headlines without being ghoulish, remain viable in reruns, and still draw 11 million viewers.

CONTINUES ON PAGE 34 ▶

THE LARRY SANDERS SHOW

24 Homeland
Showtime
(2011–present)

Hailed as an up-to-the-minute spy saga that Washington types actually watch, *Homeland* has survived some major course corrections in its relatively short lifespan (Sergeant Brody, we still miss you). Running like an electric current beneath the drama's excellent acting and dialogue is jolting, disruptive storytelling, which tricks you in the best way. This is not a TV show with a deep "mythology"—it's mass entertainment at the highest level.

25 The Larry Sanders Show
HBO (1992-98)

Ricky Gervais cites Garry Shandling's fearless Hollywood satire as an inspiration for *The Office*. We're also impressed that Shandling found cast members Rip Torn, Jeffrey Tambor, Janeane Garofalo, and Jeremy Piven back when they were cheap(er). ∎

British Imports

HERE'S A LOOK AT THE IMPORTS FROM ACROSS THE POND THAT WERE RIGHT ON TARGET—AND SOME THAT MISSED THE MARK

1	DOCTOR WHO	1963-
2	DOWNTON ABBEY	2010-
3	BLACK MIRROR	2011-
4	SHERLOCK	2010-
5	THE OFFICE	2001-2003
6	LUTHER	2010-2015
7	THE FALL	2013-
8	CALL THE MIDWIFE	2012-
9	TOP GEAR	2002-
10	EXTRAS	2005-2007
11	LIFE ON MARS	2006-2007
12	THE GRAHAM NORTON SHOW	2007-
13	ABSOLUTELY FABULOUS	1992-2012
14	COUPLING	2000-2004
15	TORCHWOOD	2006-2011
16	BROADCHURCH	2013-
17	BEING HUMAN	2008-2013
18	PEEP SHOW	2003-2015
19	SHAMELESS	2011-
20	MI-5	2002-
21	THE IT CROWD	2006-2013
22	RED DWARF	1988-
23	THE INBETWEENERS	2008-2010
24	FOYLE'S WAR	2002-2015
25	BABYLON	2014

Yes, Ricky Gervais, we're having a laugh.

23

18

16

Wherein Dame Maggie Smith casts shade

9

22

2

17

6

The small screen's Dark Knight

8

Now we know plenty 'bout birthin' babies!

20

19

3

1

4

Those lips, those eyes, that... grey matter!

Everyone needs a good Doctor.

25

11

5

7

The British version didn't end up on Mars.

24

13

14

12

21

15

WHETHER THEY LASTED ONE SEASON OR MANY, THESE BINGE-WORTHY SHOWS INSPIRE PASSIONATE REACTIONS

BUFFY THE VAMPIRE SLAYER

Buffy the Vampire Slayer

The WB (1997-2001);
UPN (2001-03)

Sarah Michelle Gellar's fully committed portrayal of the teenage vampire hunter; creator Joss Whedon's witty dialogue; the lovable ensemble; the attractive, broody vam- pires with whom Buffy kept company: They all inspired the show's fierce following, as did the fact that every one of Buffy's adventures—though filled with monsters and Big Bads—was totally relatable. (For example: Buffy sleeps with Angel, then wakes up to discover he's turned evil. Raise

← THE COMEBACK

your hand if you haven't been there.) SECRET HANDSHAKE: *"Grr! Argh!"*

2 Arrested Development

Fox (2003-06); Netflix (2013)
This critically acclaimed comedy about a privileged, self-obsessed Orange County family featured fast, delirious, interlocking jokes that don't pander to the masses; winky gags; and a cast of absurd characters. Its legend grew so powerful in cancellation that it was revived on Netflix in 2013, and a movie has been discussed as well. SECRET HANDSHAKE: *"Illusion, Michael. A trick is something a whore does for money…or candy."*

3 Mystery Science Theater 3000

KMTA (1988); The Comedy Channel (1989-91); Comedy Central (1991-96); Syfy (1997-99)
As space-traveling janitor Joel Robinson (Joel Hodgson) and later Mike Nelson heckle their way through terrible B movies along with their robot sidekicks, they taught us that snarky commentary about media can be way more entertaining than the actual media—a lesson subsequently taken to heart by *Beavis and Butt-head*, *Talk Soup*, *Tosh.0*, and every blog ever. SECRET HANDSHAKE: *"Deep Hurting."*

4 The X-Files

Fox (1993-2002)
A paean to oddballs, sci-fi fans, conspiracy theorists, and Area 51 pilgrims everywhere, *The X-Files* had a believer (David Duchovny's Fox Mulder) *versus* skeptic (Gillian Anderson's Dana Scully) dynamic that's still in heavy use on TV dramas today. SECRET HANDSHAKE: *You own a replica of Mulder's "I Want to Believe" poster.*

5 It's Always Sunny in Philadelphia

FX (2005-present)
When they're not running a dive bar in South Philadelphia, five disorderly half-wits known as "The Gang" smoke crack, get cancer, go on welfare, compose a rock opera about a pedophile troll, and kill a guy with a chain saw. If all that sounds too dark for you, there's an episode about making mittens for kittens that's adorable. SECRET HANDSHAKE: *You know every line of "The Nightman Cometh."*

6 Star Trek: The Next Generation

Syndicated (1987-94)
The original *Star Trek* was cult TV before cult TV was even a thing, but its younger, sleeker offspring—set a century after the first series—reignited the promise of sci-fi on television. SECRET HANDSHAKE: *Who's the better captain, Kirk or Picard? (Obviously, it's Picard.)*

CONTINUES ON PAGE 38 ▶

Bonus!

Shows That Replaced a Star
Two and a Half Men
NYPD Blue
Spin City
Law & Order
Beverly Hills, 90210
ER
The Daily Show
Charmed
The West Wing
The Office

Shows Set in High School
Glee
Beverly Hills, 90210
My So-Called Life
Popular
The Fresh Prince of Bel-Air
Awkward
Freaks and Geeks
Saved by the Bell
Friday Night Lights
Dawson's Creek

Actors Who've Played a Version of Themselves
Episodes,
Matt LeBlanc

Curb Your Enthusiasm,
Larry David

Louie,
Louis C.K.

Seinfeld,
Jerry Seinfeld

Don't Trust the B---- in Apt. 23,
James Van Der Beek

"I'm totally over Jordan Catalano."

7 The Comeback
HBO (2005 and 2014)

This painfully uncomfortable yet hilarious comedy was a look at a former sitcom star (played by Lisa Kudrow) trying to make a comeback (duh). It was so inside that it ran for only one season in 2005, but it had its own comeback in 2014 with a story line that brought exquisite closure to its depiction of the predatory nature of reality TV, the desperation of middle-aged female stardom, and life in the Hollywood bubble. SECRET HANDSHAKE: *"I don't want to see that!"*

8 My So-Called Life
ABC (1994-95)

Yes, it introduced the world to the tender-hearted brilliance of Claire Danes as high school sophomore Angela Chase. But more important, it was the first teen drama that didn't feel like an after-school special. And anyone who watched the show back in the '90s can now enjoy it on a very different level: Suddenly, Angela's parents are relatable. SECRET HANDSHAKE: *"Where's Tino?"*

9 Firefly
Fox (2002)

In a future where China and the United States have teamed up to colonize the galaxy by terraforming inhospitable planets, the crew of the ramshackle spaceship *Serenity* eke out a living hauling cargo and evading cannibal Reavers, intergalactic mobsters, and other threats. The sci-fi/Western mash-up, the Chinese curse words—everything that made Joss Whedon's first TV foray beyond the Buffyverse unique—also screamed "for smart nerds only." And, as it often does, martyrdom has only enhanced its legend: Fox canceled the show after airing 11 of 14 episodes produced. SECRET HANDSHAKE: *You call yourself a Browncoat.*

POP CULTURE OBSESSION

Best Super Bowl Ads

WHEN YOU'RE PAYING $4 MILLION FOR 30 SECONDS OF AIRTIME, YOU WANT YOUR VIEWERS TO FEEL AWE AND "AWWW." THESE ADS DELIVERED

Timeline: ❶ ❷❸ ❹ ❺ ❻ ❼ ❽
1990 | 1991 | 1992 | 1993 | 1994 | 1995 | 1996 | 1997 | 1998 | 1999 | 2000 | 2001

1	**DIET PEPSI** Ray Charles	1991
2	**NIKE** Michael Jordan and Bugs Bunny	1992
3	**PEPSI** "New Can," with Cindy Crawford	1992
4	**McDONALD'S** Larry Bird vs. Michael Jordan	1993
5	**BUDWEISER** Frogs	1995
6	**PEPSI** "Your Cheatin' Heart"	1996
7	**MONSTER.COM** "When I Grow Up"	1999
8	**BUDWEISER** "Respect," a 9/11 tribute	2002
9	**REEBOK** Terry Tate: Office Linebacker	2003
10	**CAREER BUILDER** "Monkey Office"	2005
11	**DORITOS** "Live the Flavor"	2007
12	**SNICKERS** Betty White	2010

BATTLESTAR GALACTICA

10 Twin Peaks
ABC (1990-91)

Set in a logging town woolly with kinky secrets, quirky locals, and otherworldly creeps, this surreal soap ran for only 30 episodes, but it was a pop phenomenon with a sensuous strangeness unique to its co-creator David Lynch (*Blue Velvet*). Look for nine new episodes from Showtime in 2017.

So say we all!

SECRET HANDSHAKE: *"Damn good coffee—and hot!"*

11 Veronica Mars
UPN (2004-06); The CW (2006-07)

It's not easy telling the story of a teen's mission to solve her best friend's murder—while also investigating her own rape—but creator Rob Thomas nailed his tough assignment by giving the smart and snarky Veronica Mars (Kristen Bell) wry one-liners to leaven the sometimes grim mysteries. A 2014 movie brought Veronica back for her 10th high school reunion and more murders to solve. SECRET HANDSHAKE: *You understand that Mars lives in Neptune.*

12 Battlestar Galactica
Syfy (2004-09)

This reboot of the short-lived sci-fi series from the late 1970s

CONTINUES ON PAGE 41 ▶

13	**GOOGLE**	2010
	"Parisian Love"	
14	**VOLKSWAGEN**	2011
	"The Force"	
15	**MOTOROLA XOOM**	2011
	"Empower the People"	
16	**NFL**	2011
	"Best Fans Ever"	
17	**OIKOS**	2012
	"The Tease," with John Stamos	
18	**BUDWEISER**	2013
	"Brotherhood"	
19	**SAMSUNG**	2013
	"The Next Big Thing"	
20	**JEEP**	2013
	"America Will be Whole Again"	
21	**BUDWEISER**	2014
	"Best Buds"	
22	**CHEERIOS**	2014
	"Gracie"	
23	**RADIO SHACK**	2014
	"The Phone Call"	
24	**ALWAYS**	2015
	"#LikeAGirl"	
25	**AVOCADOS FROM MEXICO**	2015

Bryan Cranston

SUCCESS, HE'S SAID, REQUIRES LUCK. BUT IT'S HIS LEGION OF FANS WHO ARE THE LUCKY ONES

TWELVE

EMMY NOMINATIONS

(3 for *Malcolm in the Middle*, 9 for *Breaking Bad*)

6

EMMY WINS

(all for *Breaking Bad*)

1

tattoo he has, of the Br/Ba *Breaking Bad* logo (on his right ring finger)

Breaking Bad

1.83 MILLION

Twitter followers

5

times he played dentist Tim Whatley on *Seinfeld*

10.3 MILLION

people who watched the *Breaking Bad* finale

$225,000

salary he earned per episode toward the end of *Breaking Bad*

16

age when he lost his virginity, to a "professional" while in Europe

9

months he tried doing stand-up comedy early in his career, to overcome fear

ONE

memoir he's writing, due fall 2015

1

day of the week (Monday) he didn't talk in order to rest his voice, while starring in *All the Way*

2014

year he made his Broadway debut playing Lyndon Baines Johnson in *All the Way*

1

Tony award, for *All the Way*

6'3"

LBJ's height

2"

height of lifts Cranston wore to play LBJ

10
years he didn't see his father, after his parents split when he was 12

25
pounds of bees he was covered in for episode 14, season 1, of *Malcolm in the Middle*

151
episodes of *Malcolm in the Middle*

40
age he was when his wife threw him a surprise birthday party at Dodger Stadium

62
episodes of *Breaking Bad*

186

$3 MILLION
Walter White and Jesse's salary in *Breaking Bad* from Gus Fring for three months of meth cooking

$43,700
Walter White's teacher's salary

pounds he thought Walter White should weigh at the start of *Breaking Bad*, to be "a little doughier"

2
real-life astronauts he's played (Virgil "Gus" Grissom in *That Thing You Do!* and Buzz Aldrin in *From the Earth to the Moon*)

1980
First acting appearance, uncredited, in the TV movie *To Race the Wind*

CONTINUED FROM PAGE 39

expanded the show's central premise (the search for Earth and defeat of the vengeful, synthetic Cylons) into an addictive post-9/11 parable. Stars Katee Sackhoff and Tricia Helfer became geek and feminist icons, and best of all, the show introduced this peerless profanity into the national lexicon: *Frak*! SECRET HANDSHAKE: *You can name the Final Five.*

13 Community
NBC (2009-14); Yahoo! Screen (2015-)
Technically it's about oddball community-college students who form a study group. But it's actually about seven unlikely friends—helmed by cocky ex-lawyer Jeff Winger (Joel McHale)—who spend their time parodying movies, paintballing, and occasionally exchanging romantic glances. The series' affinity for high-concept story lines, meta humor, and pop culture allusions has

earned it a fervent fan following—and got it picked up by Yahoo! Screen after NBC declined a sixth season. SECRET HANDSHAKE: *"Six seasons and a movie!"*

14 Lost
ABC (2004-10)
A plane filled with flawed souls crashes on an island, and the survivors tangle with time travel, the legacy of utopian mad scientists, and morally ambiguous Others. Initially celebrated as a character-driven drama with a humanistic worldview, *Lost* also presented itself as dramatic cryptography that demanded to be solved. Its still-debated finale was deeply meaningful to some and dissatisfying poppycock to others. SECRET HANDSHAKE: *"We have to go back!"*

15 Fringe
Fox (2008-13)

CONTINUES ON PAGE 42 ▶

seasons Supernatural *creator Eric Kripke planned the series to last; it's currently in season 11* **5**

This sci-fi drama was conceived as a procedural, with Agent Olivia Dunham (Anna Torv) and her team investigating crimes involving "fringe science." But the story lines grew more emotional and complex with the revelation of a parallel universe. SECRET HANDSHAKE: *Did Peter and Olivia really need to be a couple? Discuss.*

16 Undeclared
Fux (2001-02)

Judd Apatow's comedy about college freshmen cemented many of the Apatovian universe's central players (including Seth Rogen and Jason Segel) and got props for replacing campus clichés (nonstop partying) with more realistic concerns (the freshman 15). SECRET HANDSHAKE: *Ben Stiller explaining what "relationship" really stands for: "Real Exciting Love Affair That Turns Into Ongoing Nightmare…Sobriety Hangs in Peril…something like that; I got it tattooed on my back."*

17 Wonder Showzen
MTV2 (2005-06)

A thoroughly twisted parody of an educational children's show, *Wonder Showzen* had adorable kids saying dark, bizarre, and otherwise age-inappropriate things, often while dressed as historical figures like Hitler and "Li'l Dead Pope." You'd watch in disbelief while thinking, "Is this really happening on a network owned by a giant corporation?" SECRET HANDSHAKE: *"Who did you exploit today?"*

18 Supernatural
The WB (2005); The CW (2006-present)

This series started with a pretty straightforward premise—hot guys (brothers Dean and Sam Winchester) kill spooky things—but it didn't stay that way. The characters have literally been to hell and back, and they've woven a mythology filled with friends, foes, and inside jokes (Wincest!). The series also mocked the sillier aspects of its own existence—an approach that helped it build a hyperpassionate community. SECRET HANDSHAKE: *A fan won't take offense at being called "idjit."*

19 Popular
The WB (1999-2001)

Popular, the first show created by Ryan Murphy, was truly the proto-*Glee*, celebrating the value of high school outcasts and portraying overplayed topics—Homecoming Court, sex, and secrets—through an absurdist lens. SECRET HANDSHAKE: *"Shut your dirty whore mouth, player player!"*

TV's Most Suspenseful Episodes

TWIN PEAKS, "Lonely Souls" 1990 | **STAR TREK: THE NEXT GENERATION,** "Chain of Command: Part 2" 1992 | **ER**, "Love's Labor Lost" 1995 | **BUFFY THE VAMPIRE SLAYER**, "Innocence" 1998 | **THE X-FILES**, "Roadrunners" 2000 | **THE WIRE**, "Cleaning Up" 2002 | **THE WEST WING**, "Twenty Five" 2003 | **THE SOPRANOS**, "Long Term Parking" 2004 | **24**, "Day 5: 6:00 p.m. – 7:00 p.m." 2006 | **DESPERATE HOUSEWIVES**, "Bang" 2006 | **DEXTER**, "Born Free" 2006 | **LOST**, "Through the Looking Glass" 2007 | **GREY'S ANATOMY**, "Sanctuary" 2010 | **HOMELAND**, "Marine One" 2011 | **DOWNTON ABBEY**, season 3 episode 5—Sybil gives birth 2012 | **SONS OF ANARCHY**, "A Mother's Work" 2013 | **BREAKING BAD**, "Ozymandias" 2013 | **GAME OF THRONES**, "The Rains of Castamere" 2013 | **BLACK MIRROR**, "National Anthem" 2013 | **LAW & ORDER: SVU**, "Surrender Benson" 2013 | **THE WALKING DEAD**, "No Sanctuary" 2014 | **HANNIBAL**, "Mizumono" 2014 | **THE AMERICANS**, "EST Men" 2015 | **CASTLE**, "Reckoning" 2015 | **SCANDAL**, "Run" 2015

ARCHER

20 Party Down
Starz (2009-10)

A dream team of comedy actors—Adam Scott, Lizzy Caplan, Martin Starr, Jane Lynch, and Megan Mullally, for starters—play Hollywood wannabes slumming it as food caterers in this smart, drily funny series. SECRET HANDSHAKE: *"Are we having fun yet?"*

21 Farscape
Syfy (1999-2003)

Astronaut John Crichton (Ben Browder) accidentally flies into another universe, where he leads a band of rebels fighting baddies called Peacekeepers. If the wisecracking puppets didn't make *Farscape* cult, the silver-and-blue-alien babes surely did. SECRET HANDSHAKE: *Before* Battlestar Galactica *pop-*

ularized frak, *there was* Farscape's *frell. As in, "Why did you frelling copy us?"*

22 Better Off Ted
ABC (2009-10)

Single dad Ted Crisp (Jay Harrington) is an exec at Veridian Dynamics, where technologies like a cure for baldness (which grows hair everywhere) are created. *Ted* blended zany pep with a sly satire of corporate America— when employees are fired, a SWAT-like "Extraction Team" hunts them down. SECRET HANDSHAKE: *"Deal with it."*

23 Archer
FX (2009-present)

This viciously delightful animated James Bond spoof features rapid-fire jokes that reference everything from Burt Reynolds to Bartleby, the Scrivener ("Not a big Melville crowd here, huh? He's not an easy read"). SECRET HANDSHAKE: *You try to work "danger zone" into a conversation.*

24 Orphan Black
BBC America (2013-present)

There's no better special effect on TV than Tatiana Maslany playing a variety of clones, most working together to solve the mystery of their existence. *Orphan Black* defies any genre label, save Really Cool Original Stuff. SECRET HANDSHAKE: *"How many of us are there?"*

25 Pushing Daisies
ABC (2007-09)

Ned (Lee Pace) has two amazing talents: He makes awesome pies, and he can resurrect the dead with a touch—as long as he doesn't touch them again. The whimsy of this series polarized audiences into love-it/hate-it camps. SECRET HANDSHAKE: *You can recite the rules of Ned's power by heart.* ∎

Stars Who've Never Won an Emmy

Phylicia Rashad
Courteney Cox*
Hugh Laurie

Steve Carell
Cybill Shepherd
Jason Alexander
Calista Flockhart
Kim Cattrall
Henry Winkler
Ed O'Neill
Katey Sagal
Christopher Meloni
David Duchovny
Michael C. Hall
Denis Leary
Chris Noth*
Keri Russell*
Connie Britton
Jane Kaczmarek
George Clooney
Jennifer Garner
Lauren Graham*
Paul Reiser
Laura Dern
Angelia Lansbury

* never even nominated

The Greats

Albums

NIRVANA STRIPPED DOWN, EMINEM SHOWED
US THE REAL SLIM SHADY, AND ADELE WENT
ROLLING IN THE DEEP ON THESE STELLAR DISCS

1 The Miseducation of Lauryn Hill

Lauryn Hill (1998)

A state of the union for the young, black, and female at the end of the millennium, the ex-Fugee's five-Grammy take only confirmed the impact of her solo breakthrough, with a genre-busting blend of deep-groove retro soul, hip-hop ingenuity and intelligent song craft.

2 The Low End Theory

A Tribe Called Quest (1991)

Stuffy-nosed lothario Q-Tip and "five-foot assassin" Phife Dawg dug deep into their vinyl collections for a bouncy bebop response to gansta rap.

3 Achtung Baby

U2 (1991)

The Irish superstars' seventh studio album made a substantial leap, recognizing the emergence of alt-rock and electronic music in a way that was both ingenious and organic.

LAURYN HILL

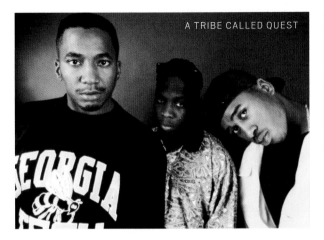

A TRIBE CALLED QUEST

4 My Beautiful Dark Twisted Fantasy

Kanye West (2010)

It starts with a question: "Can we get much higher?" After 70 thunderous minutes of hip-hop anthems, prog-rock bliss-outs, and I'ma-let-you-finish bravura, you have your answer: No. No, we cannot.

5 American Idiot

Green Day (2004)

Forget the Sex Pistols. Punk didn't truly go mainstream until these three snotty, snarling postadolescents broke through to become arena-filling icons, and with songs like "Boulevard of Broken Dreams," they proved that a little maturity can be a good thing.

6 The Blueprint

Jay-Z (2001)

Its release date—Sept. 11, 2001—couldn't have been worse, yet *The Blueprint*, featuring ingenious samples and lush production by a then-unknown Kanye West, went straight to No. 1, thanks in part to radio hits "Izzo (H.O.V.A.)" and "Girls, Girls, Girls."

7 OK Computer

Radiohead (1997)

From the jagged guitar menace of "Paranoid Android" to the grand orchestral sweep of "Karma Police," this is the sound of the biggest rock band of its time becoming the most important one.

CONTINUES ON PAGE 47 ▶

Bonus!

Best Boy Bands	Their Best Song
New Kids on the Block	"Step by Step"
Boyz II Men	"End of the Road"
Backstreet Boys	"I Want It That Way"
NSYNC	"Bye Bye Bye"
One Direction	"What Makes You Beautiful"

Best Girl Groups	Their Best Song
Wilson Phillips	"Hold On"
Destiny's Child	"Say My Name"
TLC	"Waterfalls"
Spice Girls	"Wannabe"
Dixie Chicks	"Wide Open Spaces"

Top Touring Artists		GROSS
1.	The Rolling Stones	$1.6 BILLION
2.	U2	$1.5 BILLION
3.	Bruce Springsteen	$1.2 BILLION
4.	Madonna	$1.1 BILLION
5.	Bon Jovi	$1 BILLION

U2

Kanye West

HE'S FAMOUS FOR AWARD-SHOW INTERRUPTUS, A MARRIAGE MADE IN TABLOID HEAVEN—AND AN OUTSIZE MUSICAL TALENT

$8,800
payment received for selling his first eight beats to Chicago rapper Gravity, while he was still a teen

$200
price of his Adidas Yeezy Boost sneakers

12
minutes it took for 9,000 pairs of his Yeezy Boosts 350s to sell out, via an app

$1,025
the average resale price of Yeezy Boosts 350s later online

3
the age he said he tries to think back to when he's being creative

10
how old he was when he lived in China for a year

30
koi fish he bought himself after the success of his debut album, *The College Dropout*

TWO
short films in which he served as director, actor, and writer (*Runaway*, 2010; *Cruel Summer*, 2012)

1
semester of art school attended

13.6 MILLION
Twitter followers

1
person he follows on Twitter (his wife)

2009
year he stormed the stage at the MTV Video Music Awards to interrupt Taylor Swift's acceptance speech

53
Grammy nominations

21
Grammy wins

60 height in feet of the circular LED screen crafted for his Yeezus tour in 2013

24,000 pounds the LED screen weighed

16 days his tour had to go on hiatus while trusses for the screen were repaired following a truck accident

$25.2 MILLION total gross of the Yeezus tour through December 2013, making it the year's second highest grosser

2002 year he suffered a near-fatal car crash; his song "Through the Wire" deals with that experience

2007 year his beloved mother, Donda, died from complications following plastic surgery

2015 year named one of *Time*'s 100 Most Influential People

fifteen carats in the Lorraine Schwartz diamond engagement ring Kanye gave Kardashian, estimated value **$1.25 MILLION–$4 MILLION**

$100,000+ cost of the flowers at his wedding in Florence, Italy, to Kim Kardashian

7 height in feet of the couple's wedding cake

2 altercations with a paparazzo at Los Angeles International Airport

CONTINUED FROM PAGE 45

NIRVANA

8 MTV Unplugged in New York

Nirvana (1994)

Never mind *Nevermind*. *Unplugged* captures the band raw and beautiful. Even without the stripped-down originals, the soul-scraping Lead Belly classic "Where Did You Sleep Last Night" and Bowie's "The Man Who Sold the World" marked this as a classic.

9 Stankonia

OutKast (2000)

Before "Hey Ya!" made OutKast inescapable, this album catapulted the eccentric Atlanta duo from hip-hop cult status to genuine MTV players.

10 The Marshall Mathers LP

Eminem (2000)

A millennial cherry bomb in the staid pop marketplace, this slice of the rapper's psyche contains several landmark singles ("Stan," "The Real Slim Shady," "The Way I Am").

CONTINUES ON PAGE 49 ▶

Musical Movie Moments

WAYNE'S WORLD

- **GOODFELLAS** (1990), "Layla" by Derek and the Dominos

- **WAYNE'S WORLD** (1992), "Bohemian Rhapsody" by Queen

- **RESERVOIR DOGS** (1992), "Stuck in the Middle With You" by Stealers Wheel

- **PULP FICTION** (1994), "Girl, You'll Be a Woman Soon" by Urge Overkill

- **CHUNGKING EXPRESS** (1994), "California Dreamin'" by the Mamas and the Papas

- **THE FIRST WIVES CLUB** (1996), "You Don't Own Me" by Lesley Gore

- **TRAINSPOTTING** (1996), "Lust for Life" by Iggy Pop

- **THE SWEET HERE-AFTER** (1997), "Courage" by Sarah Polley

- **MY BEST FRIEND'S WEDDING** (1997), "I Say a Little Prayer" by Diana King

- **BOOGIE NIGHTS** (1997), "Jessie's Girl" by Rick Springfield

- **THE BIG LEBOWSKI** (1998), "Just Dropped In (To See What Condition My Condition Was In)" by Kenny Rogers and the First Edition

- **FIGHT CLUB** (1999), "Where Is My Mind?" by the Pixies

- **MAGNOLIA** (1999), "Wise Up" by Aimee Mann

- **ALMOST FAMOUS** (2000), "Tiny Dancer" by Elton John

- **AMERICAN PSYCHO** (2000), "Hip to Be Square" by Huey Lewis and the News

- **DANCER IN THE DARK** (2000), "I've Seen It All" by Björk

- **THE ROYAL TENENBAUMS** (2001), "These Days" by Nico

- **DONNIE DARKO**

THE FIRST WIVES CLUB

(2001), "Head Over Heels" by Tears for Fears

- **LOVE ACTUALLY** (2003), "Jump (For My Love)" by the Pointer Sisters

- **13 GOING ON 30** (2004), "Thriller" by Michael Jackson

- **ANCHORMAN: THE LEGEND OF RON BURGUNDY** (2004), "Afternoon Delight" by Starland Vocal Band

- **ONCE** (2006), "Falling Slowly" by Glen Hansard and Markéta Irglová

- **BRIDESMAIDS** (2011), "Hold On" by Wilson Phillips

- **THE PERKS OF BEING A WALLFLOWER** (2012), "Heroes" by David Bowie

- **THE SKELETON TWINS** (2014), "Nothing's Gonna Stop Us Now" by the Jefferson Starship

BOOGIE NIGHTS

THE ROYAL TENENBAUMS

ALBUMS CONTINUED FROM PAGE 47

11 Odelay
Beck (1996)

"Loser" could have made Beck a one-hit wonder. Instead, he followed with this postmod casserole of gutter funk, lo-fi folk, loopy jazz, and clever turntablism—a perfect balance of hip disaffectedness and depth of feeling.

12 Beyoncé
Beyoncé (2013)

Surprise-released at the end of the year, Bey's self-titled Christmas gift to fans came stuffed with dreamy songs, from frank sex jams to an ode to daughter Blue Ivy, that indulge clashing impulses—between strength and escape, megapop and fresh sounds, big messages and resonant lyrics.

13 Tidal
Fiona Apple (1996)

At 18, the piano-playing nymphet already displayed a startlingly precocious talent for songwriting—and scandal (the infamous kiddie-porn-aping video "Criminal").

14 White Blood Cells
The White Stripes (2001)

This 16-song rampage of bleeding-raw guitar riffs and carnal rhythms honored the roots of blues rock while dragging it into the 21st century by the seat of its red-and-white pants.

15 The Suburbs
Arcade Fire (2010)

A work of fervent majesty, toggling between near-messianic uplift and flat-out despair, from the Canadian collective that's committed to dense and deeply felt albums.

16 Illmatic
Nas (1994)

Only 20 at the time, Nasir Jones was swiftly labeled hip-hop's Next Great MC with this mid-'90s masterwork—a richly textured urban tapestry vibrating with the rapper's keen intellect and vivid storytelling skills.

17 Discovery
Daft Punk (2001)

Just two French guys in robot helmets, pumping out electro-funk anthems so Rick James–meets–R2-D2 *magnifique*, the dance floor could hardly stand it. That it also essentially set the template for the '00s EDM explosion, which the duo would go on to gleefully subvert with their 2013 creation *Random Access Memories*, featuring "Get Lucky" as the lead single? Le bonus!

18 Is This It
The Strokes (2001)

Rock trademarks like off-kilter guitar solos, half-buried vocals, primitive tom-tom rhythms, and the raw, muddy sonics of garage-band 45s are blended into an energetic new kick that's never retro.

CONTINUES ON PAGE 50 ▶

Catchiest One-Hit Wonders

SOME ARE STILL EARWORMY, OTHERS EXCRUCIATING

"ONE OF US," Joan Osborne	1995
"YOU GET WHAT YOU GIVE," New Radicals	1998
"SOMEBODY THAT I USED TO KNOW," Gotye feat. Kimbra	2012
"YOU GOTTA BE," Des'ree	1994
"GIRL LIKE YOU," Edwyn Collins	1995
"CLOSING TIME," Semisonic	1998
"I TOUCH MYSELF," Divinyls	1990
"HEY THERE DELILAH," Plain White Ts	2006
"WHAT'S UP?," 4 Non Blondes	1993
"I'M TOO SEXY," Right Said Fred	1991
"BABY GOT BACK," Sir Mix-A-Lot	1992
"STACY'S MOM," Fountains of Wayne	2003
"STEAL MY SUNSHINE," Len	1999
"FLAGPOLE SITTA," Harvey Danger	1998
"LIPS OF AN ANGEL," Hinder	2005
"THE MIDDLE," Jimmy Eat World	2001
"REBIRTH OF SLICK (COOL LIKE DAT)," Digable Planets	1992
"CHASING CARS," Snow Patrol	2006
"TUBTHUMPING," Chumbawamba	1997
"JUMP AROUND," House of Pain	1992
"BAD DAY," Daniel Powter	2005
"YOU'RE BEAUTIFUL," James Blunt	2005
"MY NECK, MY BACK," Khia	2002
"GANGNAM STYLE," Psy	2012
"WHO LET THE DOGS OUT?," Baha Men	2000

TIMELESS — STILL ENJOYABLE — TEDIOUS

ALBUMS CONTINUED FROM PAGE 49

19 The Moon & Antarctica

Modest Mouse (2000)
The major-label debut from the Northwest indie heroes (released on CD as well as vinyl) is an angular, experimental treasure floated on the strength of spare beauties like "Gravity Rides Everything."

20 Ready to Die

The Notorious B.I.G. (1994)
"If you don't know, now you know"—Biggie, to anyone who's ever crossed paths with this East Coast rap classic. And indeed it's hard to find a first album that delivered a superstar more fully formed.

THE WHITE STRIPES

ADELE

21
Homogenic
Björk (1997)

A series of meditations on love and lovers' deficiencies, this audacious album aims to create a new hybrid from two seemingly incompatible genres, techno and classical. The results are raw, emotional, and exciting—like sneaking a boom box into a chamber music recital.

22
Exile in Guyville
Liz Phair (1993)

Phair's cagey alt-pop comes on as uncommonly intimate and "feminine" but still leaves you aching at the door, a pun in your hand and a hook in your heart.

23
21
Adele (2011)

Dude who did Adele wrong, we salute you; if you'd been at all a better man, we wouldn't have this towering contribution to the Breakup Hall of Fame. At a time when digitally tweaked vocals are everywhere, *21* features a rare thing: a singer who can seriously sing, belting out love songs inspired by another time on an album that feels genuinely timeless.

24
Fever to Tell
Yeah Yeah Yeahs (2003)

On the group's first full-length album, Karen O howls and growls her way through 37 minutes of art-school punk with enough strapped-on swagger to make Mick Jagger blush.

25
Channel Orange
Frank Ocean (2012)

If Southern California needs an avant-R&B soundtrack, let this be it. Ocean's hypnotic major-label debut plays like an indie movie, with songs about sun-faded palm trees, cokeheads in Polo sweats, and strippers in Cleopatra makeup. ∎

Videos

WHEN MEMORABLE SONGS MEET VISIONARY
MUSICIANS AND DIRECTORS, THE RESULTS CAN
BE THRILLING WORKS OF ART

MADONNA

2 Buddy Holly
Weezer (1994)

Director Spike Jonze established himself as one of the '90s greatest music video auteurs with this loving parody to the '70s show *Happy Days* that's also sarcastic in a way that's unmistakably Gen-X.

3 The Real Slim Shady
Eminem (2000)

The controversial rapper proved he was a force to be reckoned with—literally. The clip showcases Em lambasting Britney, Pam Anderson, and the press with the help of an army of imitators sporting his trademark platinum-blond buzz cut.

1 Vogue
Madonna (1990)

No one dominated the short-form music video in the '90s quite like the Queen of Pop, whether she was writhing on the beach with mermen in "Cherish" or flaunting her girl power in the sex-positive "Express Yourself." But it's her black-and-white ode to vogueing culture (a style of dance popularized by gay men in New York City) that endures the most—not to mention that infamous cone-shaped bra and her spoken-word tribute to legends ("Lauren, Katharine, Lana, too, Bette Davis, we love you!") of the Hollywood silver screen.

4 Single Ladies (Put a Ring on It)
Beyoncé (2008)

There's a reason it has more than 400 million views online: Queen B shakes, gyrates, struts, and booty-pops such

NIRVANA

undeniably fierce moves, the world is still trying to replicate them six years later.

5 Sabotage
The Beastie Boys (1994)
With New York's hip-hop group, Jonze once again created an epic lampoon: This time the director focused his camera eye on cheesy cop TV shows like *Starsky and Hutch* and *Hunter*—but it's the Beastie Boys' hilarious acting that adds an extra layer of wit.

6 November Rain
Guns N' Roses (1992)
Most gloriously ridiculous video of the '90s? It's up there—and G n' R had the million-dollar budget to prove it. Axl Rose and Co.'s epic 9-minute minimovie has it all:

a giant symphony backing the band on a soundstage, super-model Stephanie Seymour, an over-the-top wedding ruined by rain, and, of course, Slash ditching the ceremony so he could shred on an incredible solo (while a Marlboro Red dangles from his mouth, of course).

7 Smells Like Teen Spirit
Nirvana (1991)
It's the video that ignited grunge mania—from a band that couldn't care less about MTV in the first place. Almost 25 years later, Kurt Cobain and Co.'s riot in a high school gym still comes on like a refreshing blast of anarchic insanity.

CONTINUES ON PAGE 55 ▶

Bonus!

Best Singles

"VOGUE," Madonna	1990
"LOSING MY RELIGION," R.E.M.	1991
"SMELLS LIKE TEEN SPIRIT," Nirvana	1991
"LOSER," Beck	1994
"GOOD RIDDANCE (TIME OF YOUR LIFE)," Green Day	1997
"LOSE YOURSELF," Eminem	2002
"SEVEN NATION ARMY," The White Stripes	2004
"CRAZY IN LOVE," Beyoncé feat. Jay Z	2003
"HEY YA!," OutKast	2003
"SINCE U BEEN GONE," Kelly Clarkson	2004
"GOLD DIGGER," Kanye West	2005
"SEXYBACK," Justin Timberlake feat. Timbaland	2006
"REHAB," Amy Winehouse	2006
"UMBRELLA," Rihanna feat. Jay-Z	2007
"PAPER PLANES," M.I.A.	2007
"BAD ROMANCE," Lady Gaga	2009
"EMPIRE STATE OF MIND," Alicia Keys and Jay-Z	2009
"JUST THE WAY YOU ARE," Bruno Mars	2010
"SUPER BASS," Nicki Minaj	2010
"ROLLING IN THE DEEP," Adele	2011
"SOMEBODY THAT I USED TO KNOW," Gotye feat. Kimbra	2011
"I KNEW YOU WERE TROUBLE," Taylor Swift	2012
"GET LUCKY," Daft Punk feat. Pharrell Williams and Nile Rodgers	2013
"ROYALS," Lorde	2013
"STAY WITH ME," Sam Smith	2014

Madonna

IN HER 33-YEAR CAREER, SHE'S GONE FROM BEING THE MATERIAL GIRL TO THE QUEEN OF POP. LONG MAY SHE REIGN!

14
times she said the F word on *Late Show With David Letterman*, March 31, 1994

18
children's books written or co-written

1
Coffee-table sex book written, 1992's *Sex*

150,000
copies of *Sex* sold on its first day of release

1
pair of her underwear she asked Letterman to smell during her appearance

28
Grammy nominations

7
Grammy wins

85
costume changes in *Evita*, the most in any film, according to the *Guinness Book of World Records*

FOUR
years she struggled in New York before her 1982 single "Everybody" made her a star on the club scene

1990
Year nominated to receive a star on the Hollywood Walk of Fame; she wasn't interested in getting the honor

2008
year inducted into the Rock and Roll Hall of Fame

one

microscopic organism named after her: a species of Tardigrade, or "water bear," known for living in hostile environments

$520 MILLION

HER NET WORTH

27,227
average attendance at her concerts

18
feature films in which she's appeared

2
feature films she's directed

1988
year she made her Broadway debut, in *Speed-the-Plow*

$5 MILLION+
fee she pocketed to endorse Pepsi; she was dropped after the first ad— tied to her single "Like a Prayer"—was pulled due to the song's controversial video

5
foods she says she can make: eggs, pasta, coffee, sandwiches, and Rice Krispies treats

7
Golden Globe nominations

2
Golden Globe wins (Best Actress for *Evita* and Best Original Song for "Masterpiece")

300 MILLION+
RECORDS SOLD WORLDWIDE

68
MTV Video Music Award nominations

20
MTV Video Music Awards won

four
Videos Oscar-nominated director David Fincher has made with her

---

CONTINUED FROM PAGE 53

8 It's Oh So Quiet
Björk (1995)
Nothing is tranquil about this Icelandic singer's big-band anthem: Björk creates the flamboyant charm of an explosive Broadway musical in this wonderfully choreographed clip directed by Spike Jonze.

9 Scream
Michael and Janet Jackson (1995)
Two of the world's most watched (and heavily scrutinized) pop stars teaming up for one of the most expensive videos ever produced? The odds may not have been in their favor—but the Jackson siblings managed to create an unforgettable spectacle that's literally out of this world.

10 Criminal
Fiona Apple (1997)
She's been a bad, bad girl—especially in this video capturing a late-night house party made all the more titillating by director Mark Romanek's slow and steady voyeuristic camera pans.

11 Hey Ya!
OutKast (2003)
Andre 3000 and Big Boi pair the catchiest anthem of the decade with a colorful nod to the Beatles' landmark debut on *The Ed Sullivan Show.*

12 Tonight, Tonight
The Smashing Pumpkins (1996)
Inspired by George Melies' silent movie *A Trip to the Moon*, the Smashing Pumpkins evoke an immersive sci-fi world as envisioned in Victorian times.

CONTINUES ON PAGE 56 ▶

13 The Rain (Supa Dupa Fly)

Missy Elliott (1997)

Graffiti artist-turned-director Hype Williams perfectly encapsulated Missy's groundbreaking hip-hop sound by filming the songwriter (along with SWV's Taj, Lil' Kim, Da Brat and Puff Daddy) with a trippy fish-eye lens.

14 Devils Haircut

Beck (1996)

The troubadour blew up the notions of what alternative-rock could be on his groundbreaking Grammy-winning album *Odelay,* and his simple video—which tracks the singer-songwriter roaming around empty city streets with only a boombox—was the perfect way to show off Beck's bold new sound.

15 Telephone

Lady Gaga featuring Beyoncé (2010)

Gaga has said she wanted to replicate the days when video debuts were massive pop culture events—and she scored in this epic minimovie

MICHAEL AND
JANET JACKSON

that pays tribute to Quentin Tarantino's 2003 flick *Kill Bill: Vol. 1.*

16 Hypnotize

The Notorious B.I.G. (1997)

The late rapper teamed up with Puff Daddy to prove they were hip-hop ballers in this over-the-top clip showcasing yachts, sexy female dancers, motorcycles, a Hummer and more—nothing immortalizes hip-hop excess of the '90s quite like this.

17 Praise You

Fatboy Slim (1999)

Jonze (once again) laid the groundwork for the flash mob trend of the '00s in this guerilla-style clip showing nerdy dancers shimmying and shaking as puzzled onlookers look on.

18 Somebody That I Used to Know

Gotye featuring Kimbra (2011)

The Belgian-Australian singer-songwriter and collaborator Kimbra had their nude bodies painted over like a piece of museum-quality art in this scintillating stop-animation video.

19 Nothing Compares 2 U

Sinéad O'Connor (1990)

One of the most striking videos of the '90s cut so deep because of its simplicity: just the Irish siren, shot up close, crooning Prince's gut-wrenching love song to the camera. You can catch a single tear streaming down her face midway through.

20 Everlong
Foo Fighters (1997)

Michel Gondry helmed this surreal clip that took viewers inside the bizarre dreamlike world of Grohl's lovelorn punk rocker. Not only did it win an MTV Moonman for Best Video in 1998—it also introduced a humorous side that fans rarely saw during Grohl's time drumming for Nirvana.

21 Around the World
Daft Punk (1997)

Gondry, once again, brought his revolutionary eye for short-form storytelling to this clip, which captures mummies and skeletons getting their boogie on in a club. Disco, it turns out, didn't die in the '80s after all.

22 Ironic
Alanis Morissette (1996)

No sexy backup dancers or million-dollar budgets were required for the Canadian singer's smash single: Director Stephane Sednaoui's clip showcases Morissette (and three other split personalities) cruising in a beat-up '70s sedan on a chilly winter day. Sure, it wasn't ironic, but there's no denying the simple beauty of this low-budget clip.

CONTINUES ON PAGE 58 ▶

BJÖRK

Odd Couple Duets

	WONDRFULLY ODD	
"STAN," Eminem & Elton John		2001
"AIRPLANES," B.o.B. & Hayley Williams		2010
"WHERE THE WILD ROSES GROW," Nick Cave and the Bad Seeds & Kylie Minogue		1995
"FOURFIVESECONDS," Rihanna, Kanye West, & Paul McCartney		2015
"WILD NIGHT," John Mellencamp with Me'Shell Ndeg		1994
"ALL OF THIS," Blink-182 & the Cure's Robert Smith		2003
"UNFORGETTABLE," Natalie Cole & Nat "King" Cole		1991
"OVER AND OVER," Nelly & Tim McGraw		2004
"SMOOTH," Santana & Rob Thomas		1999
"MISS SARAJEVO," U2 & Luciano Pavarotti		1995
"LATCH," Disclosure & Sam Smith		2012
"PROMISCUOUS," Nelly Furtado & Timbaland		2006
"EMPIRE STATE OF MIND," Jay-Z & Alicia Keys		2009
"I'LL BE THERE FOR YOU/YOU'RE ALL I NEED TO GET BY," Mary J. Blige and Method Man		1995
"DILEMMA," Nelly & Kelly Rowland		2002
"JUSTIFIED AND ANCIENT," The KLF & Tammy Wyn		1992
"THUG STORY," Taylor Swift & T-Pain		2009
"PORTLAND OREGON," Loretta Lynn & Jack White		2004
"ME AGAINST THE MUSIC," Britney Spears and Mad		2003
"WHATTA MAN," Salt-n-Pepa & En Vogue	JUST MAKES SENSE	1993
"PICTURE," Kid Rock & Sheryl Crow		2002
"THE BOY IS MINE," Brandy & Monica		1998
"NIGGAS IN PARIS," Kanye West & Jay-Z		2011
"JUST GIVE ME A REASON," Pink & Nate Ruess		2013
"REGULATE," Warren G & Nate Dogg		1994

VIDEOS CONTINUED FROM PAGE 57

23 Closer
Nine Inch Nails (1994)

The industrial rock group's video was one of the most controversial of the '90s—and one of the most weirdly alluring. Director Mark Romanek's sepia-toned visuals take viewers into a twisted mad scientist's lab, complete with S&M imagery, turn-of-the-century medical ephemera, a monkey tethered to a wooden cross, and NIN frontman Trent Reznor bound and gagged as a blindfolded bondage slave.

24 Seven Nation Army
The White Stripes (2003)

Jack and Meg White's thumping anthem is the short-form equivalent of falling down a kaleidoscopic rabbit hole.

25 Come to Daddy
Aphex Twin (1997)

Director Chris Cunningham pays tribute to Stanley Kubrick's *A Clockwork Orange* in this gritty, terrifying chronicle of kiddie riots in a British working-class slum. ∎

THE WHITE STRIPES

THE BULLSEYE

Summer Anthems

HERE'S A LOOK AT THE SIZZLING ANTHEMS THAT WERE RIGHT ON TARGET—AND SOME THAT MISSED THE MARK

1	"CALIFORNIA GURLS," Katy Perry feat. Snoop Dogg	2010
2	"ALL I WANNA DO," Sheryl Crow	1994
3	"RUN-AROUND," Blues Traveler	1995
4	"LIVIN' LA VIDA LOCA," Ricky Martin	1999
5	"PROBLEM," Ariana Grande feat. Iggy Azalea	2014
6	"I GOTTA FEELING," The Black Eyed Peas	2009
7	"BABY GOT BACK," Sir Mix-a-Lot	1992
8	"VIVA LA VIDA," Coldplay	2008
9	"MMMBOP," Hanson	1997
10	"WATERFALLS," TLC	1995
11	"STEP BY STEP," New Kids on the Block	1990
12	"CALL ME MAYBE," Carly Rae Jepsen	2012
13	"SUMMERTIME," DJ Jazzy Jeff & The Fresh Prince	1991
14	"TENNESSEE," Arrested Development	1992
15	"STAY (I MISSED YOU)," Lisa Loeb	1994
16	"WHOOMP! THERE IT IS," Tag Team	1993
17	"EVERYBODY," Backstreet Boys	1998
18	"HOT IN HERRE," Nelly	2002
19	"IT'S FIVE O'CLOCK SOMEWHERE," Alan Jackson and Jimmy Buffett	2003
20	"HOLLABACK GIRL," Gwen Stefani	2005
21	"CRAZY," Gnarls Barkley	2006
22	"HIPS DON'T LIE," Shakira	2006
23	"MACARENA (BAYSIDE BOYS MIX)," Los Del Rio	1996
24	"PARTY ROCK ANTHEM," LMFAO	2011
25	"BLURRED LINES," Robin Thicke and Pharrell Williams	2013

I like a good beer buzz
early in the morning.

A critique of the narrow-
minded and narrow-hipped
standard of female beauty

Katy, we'll always
party with you.

The shiniest piece of
candy in 2012's sugar-
rush pop pile

Go ahead, put your
pom-poms down

MIRANDA LAMBERT
"The House That Built Me"
(2009)

ERIC CHURCH
"Springsteen"
(2011)

TIM MCGRAW
"Live Like You Were Dying"
(2004)

NOSTALGIA

COUNTRY PLEASURE

BRAD PAISLEY
"Letter to Me" (2007)

LEE ANN WOMACK
WITH SONS OF THE DESERT
"I Hope You Dance" (2000)

LIVING LIFE TO THE FULLEST

POP CULTURE OBSESSION

Country Songs

FROM THE POIGNANT TO THE
PARTY-HEARTY, THESE 25 GREAT
TUNES TAP INTO MANY OF THE
CLASSIC COUNTRY MUSIC THEMES

KACEY MUSGRAVES
"Merry Go Round"
(2013)

DIXIE CHICKS
"Wide Open Spaces"
(1998)

FAITH HILL
"This Kiss"
(1998)

KEITH URBAN
"Somebody Like You"
(2002)

NEW LOVE

LOVE

LUKE BRYAN
"Drink a Beer"
(2013)

RASCAL FLATTS
"Bless the
Broken Road"
(2004)

GARTH BROOKS
"The Dance"
(1989)

LOVERS OR FRIENDS LOST

ALAN JACKSON
"Don't Rock the Jukebox"
(1991)

CARRIE
UNDERWOOD
"Before He
Cheats"
(2005)

MARTINA
McBRIDE
"Independence
Day" (1993)

REVENGE

SHANIA TWAIN
you're still the one

DIAMOND RIO
"Meet in the Middle"
(1991)

FLORIDA
GEORGIA LINE
"Cruise"
(2012)

SHANIA TWAIN
"You're Still the One"
(1998)

LASTING PASSION

LADY ANTEBELLUM
"Need You Now"
(2010)

DRIVING

JASON ALDEAN
"Big Green Tractor"
(2009)

DRINKING

Where Were You
(When the World Stopped Turning)

KENNY CHESNEY
"Summertime"
(2005)

ALAN JACKSON
"Where Were You (When
the World Stopped Turning)"
(2002)

summertime
kenny chesney

TOBY KEITH
"Courtesy of the Red,
White and Blue (The Angry
American)" (2002)

GRETCHEN WILSON
"Redneck Woman"
(2004)

PATRIOTISM

GRETCHEN WILSON

REDNECK WOMAN

LITTLE TEXAS
"God Blessed Texas"
(1993)

Books

1 The Road
Cormac McCarthy (2006)

A father and son trudge across an ashen American landscape in the wake of some unnamed apocalypse, fighting off sexually predatory bandits, scavenging for food, uncovering charnel-house horrors, then moving on, constantly moving on, toward some mirage of a better future. We don't need writers of Cormac McCarthy's caliber to inform us of looming planetary catastrophes; we can read the newspaper for that. We need McCarthy to imagine the fate of the human soul if the worst really does come to pass; what he depicts in *The Road* is strange, awful, tender, and, in the end, surprising.

2 The Brief Wondrous Life of Oscar Wao
Junot Díaz (2007)

Díaz creates his own language—a vigorous high-low street Spanglish—to write about Oscar, the tubby sci-fi geek hero from a Dominican immigrant family. Oscar's clan has experienced a long run of terrible luck, and their misfortunes typically begin with sex. When the hapless protagonist is sucked into the erotic maelstrom, he momentarily changes its current, emerging as an unlikely hero. Oscar's story is indeed brief, but, like this novel, it is also quite wondrous.

3 The Liars' Club
Mary Karr (1995)

Mother was much married and "Nervous." Daddy liked to

Book-to-Screen Adaptations

READ THE BOOK OR WATCH THE MOVIE?
LET OUR RANKING HELP YOU DECIDE

THE HARRY POTTER SERIES
J.K. Rowling

| BOOK | ——————O |
| MOVIES | —O———— |

LIFE OF PI
Yann Martel

| BOOK | ————O— |
| MOVIE | —O———— |

THE SILENCE OF THE LAMBS
Thomas Harris

| BOOK | —O———— |
| MOVIE | ——————O |

GAME OF THRONES
George R.R. Martin

| BOOK | ————O— |
| SERIES | ————O— |

THE HUNGER GAMES SERIES
Suzanne Collins

| BOOK | ———O—— |
| MOVIES | ——O——— |

drink. Their home in East Texas was definitely "Not Right." The dysfunctional childhood is now a staple of memoirs, but no one has handled the material with more artistry and wit.

4 Behind the Beautiful Forevers

Katherine Boo (2012)
An extraordinary feat of reporting and compassion,

Behind the Beautiful Forevers is the story of an Indian slum that plays out like a Dickens novel. Is it painful to read? Sure. A lot of unforgettable things are.

5 The Emperor of All Maladies

Siddhartha Mukherjee (2010)
A riveting history of the disease that cancer researcher

CONTINUES ON PAGE 65 ▶

Bonus!

Best Food Books

TENDER AT THE BONE	Ruth Reichl
HEAT	Bill Buford
THE MAN WHO ATE EVERYTHING	Jeffrey Steingarten
JULIE & JULIA	Julie Powell
KITCHEN CONFIDENTIAL	Anthony Bourdain
BLOOD, BONES & BUTTER	Gabrielle Hamilton
FAST FOOD NATION	Eric Schlosser
THE OMNIVORE'S DILEMMA	Michael Pollan
TOAST	Nigel Slater
INSATIABLE	Gael Greene

Best Books About Hollywood

THE DEVIL'S CANDY	Julie Salamon
EASY RIDERS, RAGING BULLS	Peter Biskind
YOU'LL NEVER EAT LUNCH IN THIS TOWN AGAIN	Julia Phillips
THE KID STAYS IN THE PICTURE	Robert Evans
PICTURES AT A REVOLUTION	Mark Harris

Best Audio Books

THE HARRY POTTER SERIES	read by Jim Dale
TO KILL A MOCKINGBIRD	read by Sissy Spacek
PADDINGTON HERE AND NOW	read by Stephen Fry
BLOOD ON SNOW	read by Patti Smith
THE HELP	read by Octavia Spencer and others

Best Serial-Killer Novels

AMERICAN PSYCHO	Bret Easton Ellis
THE DEXTER SERIES	Jeff Lindsay
INTENSITY	Dean Koontz
THE SHINING GIRLS	Lauren Beukes
THE ALIENIST	Caleb Carr

Stephen King

ALL HAIL UNCLE STEVIE (AS HE CALLED HIMSELF IN HIS LONGTIME *EW* COLUMN), A PROFOUNDLY PROLIFIC SCARE-MEISTER

19
number that occurs throughout his *The Dark Tower* saga

45
years he's been working on *The Dark Tower* saga

300 MILLION+
BOOKS HE'S SOLD

1,200-1,500 WORDS HE WRITES EVERY DAY

1985 year he's said he stopped worrying about money

1
sequel he wrote to 1977's *The Shining: Dr. Sleep,* published in 2013

4-F

designation he received from the draft board in 1970, declaring him unfit for service due to flat feet, punctured eardrums, and more

18
movies and TV shows he's appeared in

2
times he's appeared as himself

2
age he was when his father left the family

13

number he's afraid of (a syndrome known as triskaidekaphobia)

7
books he's written under the pseudonym Richard Bachman

$23,500 total he earned in two appearances on *Celebrity Jeopardy!* in 1995 and 1998, benefiting the Bangor YMCA and the Bangor Public Library

$2,500

advance he got for *Carrie*, published 1974

thirty

times *Carrie* was turned down before it was published

$200,000

amount he got for the paperback rights to *Carrie*

$700-$1,200

estimated value of a first edition copy of *Carrie*

3

radio stations he and wife Tabitha own in Maine: classic rock station WKIT, adult alternative WZLO, and talk/sports station WZON

1

musical he's written with John Mellencamp, *The Ghost Brothers of Darkland County*

$17 MILLION

ESTIMATED EARNINGS IN 2014

$35

payment he got for "The Glass Floor," his first professional short story sale, in 1967

2003

year he was awarded the National Book Foundation Medal for Distinguished Contribution to American Letters

159

bylines in *Entertainment Weekly*

year he was hit by a minivan while out walking, causing multiple injuries; he still walks with a slight limp

---

CONTINUED FROM PAGE 63

and physician Mukherjee calls "the defining plague of our generation," this book is crammed with fascinating characters, two of whom stand out: Sidney Farber, the man who invented modern chemotherapy, and Mary Lasker, the philanthropist who backed him. Threaded throughout are the moving tales of Mukherjee's own patients.

6 Selected Stories

Alice Munro (1996)
For more than 45 years, Munro has steadily churned out stunning short stories that read like compressed novels, conveying the sweep of a lifetime in a paragraph.

7 The Things They Carried

Tim O'Brien (1990)
James Frey could have learned from O'Brien, who openly marries fiction with autobiographical fact in his inspired stab at

deeper truths about the Vietnam War.

8 Tenth of December

George Saunders (2013)
These short stories are all about the limits of empathy: A mother struggles to do the right thing when adopting a puppy from a troubled family; a prisoner who's subjected to psychological experiments must decide whether he'll torture a fellow lab rat. Stylistically innovative, with a sharp humor that somehow makes everything sadder, this isn't just a tender, witty book. It's a guide to being human.

9 Into Thin Air

Jon Krakauer (1997)
On May 10, 1996, Krakauer scaled Mount Everest. Eight other climbers lost their lives that day. Less than one year later, the guilt-ridden author re-

CONTINUES ON PAGE 66 ▶

Bag End, Bilbo Baggin's house in Lord of the Rings, *was made twice. One was 33% smaller and used for scenes with Ian McKellen's Gandalf.*

33%

leased his searingly honest account, one of the best adventure books ever.

10 The Immortal Life of Henrietta Lacks
Rebecca Skloot (2010)

In 1951, shortly before a virulent cancer killed her, Henrietta Lacks' doctors in the "colored" ward at Johns Hopkins took a tissue sample from her cervix and sent it to the lab. Since then, her robust HeLa cells have been cited in 60,000 scientific papers, and while scientists and drug companies have profited, Lacks' children grew up hungry and, in a cruel irony given the circumstances, unable to afford health insurance. Journalist Rebecca Skloot's recounting is a tour de force—a story of modern medicine, bioethics, and race relations.

11 Black Water
Joyce Carol Oates (1992)

In just 154 pages, Oates delivers a knockout punch of a novel inspired by Chappaquiddick, the archetypal story of an idealistic woman done in by the carelessness of a powerful man.

12 A Heartbreaking Work of Staggering Genius
Dave Eggers (2000)

The magazines, the literacy centers, the efforts for Sudanese refugees: The whole McSweeney's phenomenon started with Eggers' mischie-

vous, affecting memoir about raising his kid brother at age 21 after the death of their parents.

13 Bring Up the Bodies
Hilary Mantel (2012)

This masterful re-creation of court politics in Tudor England turns Thomas Cromwell, the powerful adviser to Henry VIII who's conventionally seen as a villain, into a complicated and fascinating antihero.

14 On Beauty
Zadie Smith (2005)

A rich, old-fashioned novel

BOOK-TO-SCREEN ADAPTATIONS

THE GREAT GATSBY
F. Scott Fitzgerald

BOOK	
MOVIE	

JOHN ADAMS
David McCullough

BOOK	
MOVIE	

THE PERKS OF BEING A WALLFLOWER
Stephen Chbosky

BOOK	
MOVIE	

THE LORD OF THE RINGS SERIES
J.R.R. Tolkien

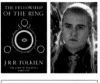

BOOK	
MOVIES	

THE DEVIL WEARS PRADA
Lauren Weisberger

BOOK	
MOVIE	

about contemporary cultural politics, this plummy saga about a mixed-race family in New England is the third—and finest—book by the gifted British author. It's 443 pages, but you wish it were longer.

Pride and Prejudice
JANE AUSTEN

15 Billy Lynn's Long Halftime Walk

Ben Fountain (2012)
On Thanksgiving 2004, a group of soldiers is reaching the end of a trip home for a hasty PR tour—culminating in a halftime appearance with Destiny's Child at a Dallas Cowboys game—after an act of bravery has turned them into instant heroes. Fountain captures the disorienting parallel realities of modern warfare: How can American life in all its glorious strangeness march on unhindered while on the other side of the world our young sol-diers grapple with unspeak-able horrors?

16 On Writing

Stephen King (2000)
When he wasn't cranking out pop classics like *The Shining*, King was battling alcoholism and the effects of a 1999 car ac-cident. He recounts both good times and bad in this memoir, which boasts his tautest writ-ing—and some of the soundest advice to writers set to paper.

17 Blindness

José Saramago (1995)
An unforgettable fable about a city in the grip of a blindness epidemic. The good news: It's riveting. The bad news: This portrait of how mankind re-sponds to desperate circum-stances . . . well, it ain't togetherness. Saramago won the Nobel Prize for a reason.

18 Columbine

Dave Cullen (2009)
Dylan Klebold and Eric Harris, both frequently portrayed in the media as black-clad goth loners, were, it turns out, pret-ty normal kids in many ways,

CONTINUES ON PAGE 68 ▶

PRIDE & PREJUDICE
Jane Austen

BOOK	———O—
SERIES	———O—

WINTER'S BONE
Daniel Woodrell

BOOK	——O——
MOVIE	—O————

NEVER LET ME GO
Kazuo Ishiguro

BOOK	——O———
MOVIE	—O————

THE GIRL WITH THE DRAGON TATTOO
Stieg Larsson

BOOK	——O———
MOVIE	——O———

THE CHRONICLES OF NARNIA: THE LION, THE WITCH AND THE WARDROBE C.S. Lewis

BOOK	——O———
MOVIE	——O———

kids with plenty of friends, certainly not the kinds of kids you'd imagine shooting up their school. How they plotted and carried out the killings at Columbine High School, and why, reads like the grisliest of fiction. Would that it were.

19 The God of Small Things

Arundhati Roy (1997)
When the daughter of one of India's declining feudal houses has an affair with an untouchable, half a dozen lives are destroyed. Roy builds small, savory details (armpits, belly buttons, insects, toys) into a Salman Rushdie-style mock epic about love across the bar of caste. All is filtered through the eyes of 7-year-old twins, who speak a private language of nicknames and repetitions. If the tale is tragic, the telling is playful, exuberant, and teeming with life.

20 Middlesex

Jeffrey Eugenides (2002)
Nothing is simple in this novel that spans generations and genders to tell the story of Cal, née Calliope, a hermaphrodite raised as a girl who was "reborn" as a genetic boy in adolescence. Now a man of 41, Cal spins his own Greek myth of how a she became a he, tracing it back to the time when his grandparents escaped the Turkish ransack of Smyrna and married, even though they were brother and sister. A vibrantly strange and heroic tale about roots and rootlessness.

21 Bel Canto

Anne Patchett (2001)
A South American embassy throws a birthday bash for a Japanese electronics mogul. A famed opera singer is on the guest list. The terrorists who swarm in through the air-conditioning vents are not. The diva's performance works miracles even with the terrorists, but it's Patchett who really sings.

22 Life After Life

Kate Atkinson (2013)

BOOK-TO-SCREEN ADAPTATIONS

THE SHAWSHANK REDEMPTION
Stephen King

BOOK		
MOVIE		

WILD
Cheryl Strayed

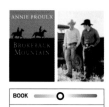

BOOK		
MOVIE		

NO COUNTRY FOR OLD MEN
Cormac McCarthy

BOOK		
MOVIE		

GONE GIRL
Gillian Flynn

BOOK		
MOVIE		

JURASSIC PARK
Michael Crichton

BOOK		
MOVIE		

number of books Cheryl Strayed read while she was walking the Pacific Crest Trail—including Lolita *and* As I Lay Dying

13

Life After Life is an utter original: a dazzlingly inventive and deeply human story about Ursula, an otherwise ordinary British girl in the first half of the 20th century who is reborn over and over again. Do her reincarnations serve a higher purpose? Is she really trying to kill Hitler? Atkinson's brilliant novel is both postmodern sleight of hand and old-fashioned storytelling in the best, most enveloping sense.

23 **Interpreter of Maladies**

Jhumpa Lahiri (1999)

The stories in Lahiri's slim but sublime Pulitzer Prize–winning collection focus on India: stair sweepers in Calcutta and emigres in New England, the gilded silk of saris and pungent scents of paprika and prunes. They read like lucid daydreams, and they revolve around communication—misinterpreted gestures, unexpressed longings, and the occasional shocking connection.

24 **Five Days at Memorial**

Sheri Fink (2013)

This riveting account of events at New Orleans' Memorial Medical Center after Hurricane Katrina slammed the city raises critical questions about bioethics, race, class, and for-profit hospitals. Fink takes us through the storm and its aftermath hour by hour, then chronicles the state's investigation into whether some patients among the 45 who died had been euthanized. When you finish the book, you'll know exactly what happened at Memorial—and why.

25 **Wild**

Cheryl Strayed (2012)

This isn't just a memoir about one woman's solo hike across 1,100 miles of the Pacific Crest Trail. It's also about survival. And whether that means finding the strength to get through a divorce, a mother's death, and a struggle with heroin (as Strayed did), or facing extreme dehydration, rattlesnakes, and bears, *Wild* offers the best life lesson of all: Whenever you think you can't go on, all you have to do is keep walking. ■

THE WALKING DEAD
Robert Kirkman, Tony Moore

| BOOK | ○ |
| MOVIE | ○ |

THE GOLDEN COMPASS
Philip Pullman

| BOOK | ○ |
| MOVIE | ○ |

EAT PRAY LOVE
Elizabeth Gilbert

| BOOK | ○ |
| MOVIE | ○ |

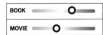

L.A. CONFIDENTIAL
James Ellroy

| BOOK | ○ |
| MOVIE | ○ |

INTO THE WILD
Jon Krakauer

| BOOK | ○ |
| MOVIE | ○ |

YA Novels

J.K. ROWLING

1 The Harry Potter Series

J.K. Rowling

He was born in Britain, but he belongs to all of us now, young and old. It's the series that enchanted a generation. Over the last decade, children—and adults—have wept over Harry's murdered parents, memorized the intimate details of owl posts, and learned to fear the dangerous nature of Horcruxes. Racism, immigration, terrorism, corruption, the war on terror, national disasters: It's all there … right alongside the grindylows and hippogriffs.

2 The Absolutely True Diary of a Part-Time Indian

Sherman Alexie

Arnold "Junior" Spirit often hitchhikes 22 miles from his Spokane Indian reservation to a local white school. Everyone resents him: his tribesmen, best friend, and new classmates. His struggle with dueling identities, plus some scatological humor, lends new life to the minority-experience narrative.

3 The Book Thief

Markus Zusak

The Nazi-era-set story presents reading as a survival mechanism—a lifeline to hope.

4 Speak

Laurie Halse Anderson

Anderson's touching novel about the aftermath of a sexual assault touched off a nationwide debate about censorship in 2010. Her publisher, Penguin, took out an ad in *The New York Times* in support of the novel.

5 Monster

Walter Dean Myers

This novel about a Harlem teen on trial for murder shows how life can hinge on just one bad choice.

6 Holes
Louis Sachar

A surreal mash-up of mystery and humor at a juvenile correctional camp—serious and seriously funny.

7 Wonder
R.J. Palacio

Born with a severe facial deformity, 10-year-old Auggie Pullman leaves the comforts of homeschooling and braves mainstream Beecher Prep.

8 Looking for Alaska
John Green

A teen guy who likes to memorize the last words of famous dead people attends boarding school in Alabama and falls for a girl named Alaska.

9 The Hunger Games
Suzanne Collins

Young people, selected by lottery, slaughter one another with kill-or-be-killed desperation, a yearly ritual broadcast on live TV and mandated by the tyrannical regime of Panem, a broken nation built on the futuristic ruins of North America. Everything changes when Katniss Everdeen volunteers for the 74th annual game.

10 A Series of Unfortunate Events
Lemony Snicket

The darkly funny mock-gothic series resists providing easy answers to its mysteries.

11 Uglies
Scott Westerfeld

In this post-apocalyptic world, looks determine the social order. At 16, citizens endure extreme plastic surgery to become part of the "Pretty" class.

12 Boy Meets Boy
David Levithan

Taking on the standard romantic plotline, Levithan's novel explores the gay community through a teenager's eyes.

13 The House of the Scorpion
Nancy Farmer

This sci-fi epic about a young clone named Matt who seeks his own fate and humanity created a menacing and unforgettable dystopian world.

14 The Sisterhood of the Traveling Pants
Anne Brashares

High school BFFs share thrift-store jeans, a metaphor for another shared experience: growing up.

15 Simon vs. the Homo Sapiens Agenda
Becky Albertalli

Sixteen-year-old Simon Spier is goaded out of the closet after a classmate discovers his emails to a pen pal.

16 Graceling
Kristin Cashore

A classic high fantasy coming-of-age adventure featuring a teenage heroine who discovers she has a special power, or Grace.

17 The House on Mango Street
Sandra Cisneros

Told through a series of vignettes, this American Book Award winner follows Esperanza Cordero, a young Latina girl looking to escape the hardships of her Latino neighborhood.

18 Stargirl
Jerry Spinelli

High schooler Leo Borlock

CONTINUES ON PAGE 73 ▶

John Green

HIS GENIUS FOR CHANNELING TEENAGERS' THOUGHTS AND EMOTIONS HAS WON HIM MILLIONS OF FANS. NOW HE'S USING HIS CELEBRITY FOR AWESOME CHARITY WORK

     five BOOKS PUBLISHED

*with David Levithan

$8,000
payment for his first novel, 2005's *Looking for Alaska*

5
months he worked as a student chaplain in a children's hospital—a later inspiration for *The Fault in Our Stars*

150,000
PRE-ORDERED COPIES OF *THE FAULT IN OUR STARS* HE SIGNED, RESULTING IN A NEED FOR SOME PHYSICAL THERAPY

11 million+
Copies of *The Fault in Our Stars* sold worldwide

47
languages *The Fault in Our Stars* has been translated into

1
cameo scene he had in *The Fault in Our Stars*, which was deleted

$12 million
budget of *The Fault in Our Stars* movie

100
percentage of days he says he cried while on the set of *The Fault in Our Stars* movie

$307 MILLION
worldwide box office gross of *The Fault in Our Stars*

17
cities visited on his 2012 bus tour

$9 million
estimated earnings in 2014

2014 the year he was named one of *Time's* 100 most influential people in the world

90
percentage of his first drafts he estimates he chucks

1 billion+

VIEWS OF HIS AND HIS BROTHER HANK'S YOUTUBE CHANNEL, VLOGBROTHERS

32
channels on
vlogbrothers

7,236
videos on
vlogbrothers

7.2 MILLION
subscribers to
vlogbrothers

4.42 MILLION
followers of his Twitter
feed @johngreen

👍 Like

3 MILLION
Facebook likes

84,200
followers of the
Twitter feed
@sportswithjohn,
where he posts
about British
football

$1.2 MILLION+
amount reportedly raised in
2014 for charity via his and Hank's
Project for Awesome and
their Foundation to
Decrease World Suck

2,800+
SIZE OF
SELL-OUT
AUDIENCE THAT
SAW HIS
EVENING
OF AWESOME
AT CARNEGIE
HALL IN 2013

1,400
attendees at
VidCon 2010,
the convention
he started

180,000
attendees at
VidCon 2015

CONTINUED FROM PAGE 71

meets a free-spirited student named Susan "Stargirl" Caraway, who ends up changing him and their high school forever.

19 The Perks of Being a Wallflower

Stephen Chbosky

Follow Charlie through his high school experience via letters he writes to an anonymous stranger.

20 Thirteen Reasons Why

Jay Asher

This humane portrait of a tormented teenager, told through a series of recordings sent to a friend, begins with suicide and only gets darker.

21 The Curious Incident of the Dog in the Night-Time

Mark Haddon

This introspective novel begins as a mystery regarding the death of a dog.

22 The Mis-education of Cameron Post

Emily Danforth

This teenage lesbian's search for sexual identity in Montana takes on epic resonance for LGBT youth.

23 Feed

M.T. Anderson

In the near future, 73 percent of citizens are hardwired to the feednet.

24 I'll Give You the Sun

Jandy Nelson

The blazing story of once inseparable twins whose lives are torn apart.

25 Code Name Verity

Elizabeth Wein

This World War II–set novel tells the same story from two points of view: a British pilot and a spy. To say much more would give away the many twists, but suffice it to say, things aren't as they seem. ■

Character Studies

Settle in as we celebrate the bravest, scariest, funniest, and smartest personalities we came to know and love—along with the era's greatest vampires, spies, presidents, detectives, and other pop culture obsessions. Plus: our favorite animated characters, screen couples, and actors' transformations.

Superheroes

THE 25 GREATEST CRIME-FIGHTERS THRILL, OCCASIONALLY KILL, AND ALWAYS KEEP THE UNIVERSE CHILL

When we set out to rank the best heroes of all time, it occurred to us: You can have a great Batman and also a really awful Batman. So instead of just listing the generic characters, we specify which version of each hero stands above the rest. Hence some icons appear more than once. For each entry, we credit the person (or persons) whose vision seems to have really made the difference.

1 Spider-Man
Stan Lee and Steve Ditko

Spidey was perhaps the first comic-book hero who wasn't so different from readers. Lee and Ditko's 1962 webslinger reinvented the muscle-bound superhero as young, funny, geeky, struggling, and flawed. The timeless life lesson that glues him together—"With great power comes great responsibility"—has never been stickier with relevance.

SPIDEY'S FIRST APPEARANCE

2 Batman
Frank Miller

Miller's 1987 comic series *Year One* has cast its dark, sinister shadow over every Batman iteration since. It's practically a superhero Western, as the lawman (and future commissioner) Jim Gordon and the outlaw vigilante (wearing a bat suit) joined forces to clean the human scum from Gotham's crime-infested streets.

3 Buffy the Vampire Slayer
Joss Whedon

Whedon created a TV Buffy who was super *and* human— and as quick with a quip as she was with a stake. Played with great verve by Sarah Michelle Gellar from 1997 to 2003, Buffy was a teen first. Her secret identity was her heroism. She vanquished a parade of Hellmouth horrors, and we salute her.

4 Iron Man
Robert Downey Jr.

With 2008's *Iron Man*, Downey took the uptight, law-and-order-oriented Tony Stark and made him Hugh Hefner in a cooler suit. Tack on the aching wisdom that Downey's age (and eyes) brings to the role, and you have the fully charged heart of the Marvel movie universe.

5 Superman
Christopher Reeve

Reeve's 1978 performance imbued the Kryptonian transplant with a salt-of-the-earth humility. Most memorable was his playful take on alter ego Clark Kent, depicting him as the meek, benign bumbler that any true superbeing would consider a spot-on impersonation of a human.

CONTINUES ON PAGE 78 ▶

Sidekicks
POP CULTURE'S TOP SECOND BANANAS

CHARACTER	SIDEKICK TO	SHOW OR MOVIE
GEORGE COSTANZA	Jerry Seinfeld	**SEINFELD**
GARY WALSH	Selina Meyer	**VEEP**
WALTER SOBCHAK	Jeffrey "The Dude" Lebowski	**THE BIG LEBOWSKI**
GROMIT	Wallace	**THE WALLACE AND GROMIT FILMS**
GARTH ALGAR	Wayne Campbell	**WAYNE'S WORLD**
MINI-ME	Dr. Evil	**THE AUSTIN POWERS FILMS**
PEDRO SANCHEZ	Napoleon Dynamite	**NAPOLEON DYNAMITE**
JOSEPH "BLUE" PULASKI	the guys of Lambda Epsilon Omega	**OLD SCHOOL**
HANK KINGSLEY	Larry Sanders	**THE LARRY SANDERS SHOW**
SILENT BOB	Jay	**THE KEVIN SMITH FILMS**
DWIGHT SCHRUTE	Michael Scott	**THE OFFICE**
RANDY HICKEY	Earl Hickey	**MY NAME IS EARL**
LANE KIM	Rory Gilmore	**GILMORE GIRLS**
WAYLON SMITHERS	C. Montgomery Burns	**THE SIMPSONS**
JESSE PINKMAN	Walter White	**BREAKING BAD**
PAUL SHAFFER	David Letterman	**LATE SHOW WITH DAVID LETTERMAN**
DONKEY	Shrek	**THE SHREK FILMS**
TURTLE	Vincent Chase	**ENTOURAGE**
DR. WATSON	Sherlock Holmes	**SHERLOCK**
GABRIELLE	Xena	**XENA: WARRIOR PRINCESS**
WILLOW ROSENBERG	Buffy Summers	**BUFFY THE VAMPIRE SLAYER**
GROOT	Rocket	**GUARDIANS OF THE GALAXY**
RON WEASLEY AND HERMIONE GRANGER	Harry Potter	**THE HARRY POTTER FILMS**
SAMWISE GAMGEE	Frodo Baggins	**THE LORD OF THE RINGS FILMS**

COMEDIC

BADASS

BATMAN

6 Wonder Woman
Lynda Carter

The show ran only from 1975 to '79, but Carter's Wonder Woman has endured in the heart of every girl who ever pretended to twirl into the dashing, daring, and brave heroine. Her greatest strength was internal—although the high-heeled red boots were pretty cool too.

7 Batman
Christopher Nolan

Director Nolan's *Dark Knight* trilogy (2005–12) liberated the hero from his campy cinematic baggage by fashioning him into a timely metaphor for morally murky justice. Christian Bale made you buy Bruce Wayne's mad fix for a mad world and then made you feel his true want: to be freed from it.

8 X-Men
Chris Claremont and John Byrne

Writer Chris Claremont and co-writer/artist John Byrne's beloved 1977–81 run with Marvel's mutant superteam showcased an ad hoc dysfunctional family whose occasional infighting was as dramatic as any high-stakes battle—and propelled Wolverine into the ranks of comicdom's surliest good guys.

9 Black Panther
Don McGregor

The noble, fearsome ruler of the fictional African nation of Wakanda became the first black superhero, debuting in 1966, but also pioneered the graphic novel in the early 1970s with writer McGregor's sensational "Panther's Rage" multi-issue story line.

10 Captain America
Ed Brubaker

What made comic scribe Brubaker's acclaimed 2005–12 run so striking was that Cap fought for a country that was often at war with itself. He faced real issues of the day not only as a hero but as the conscience of a divided nation.

CONTINUES ON PAGE 80 ▶

Political Science

THESE 25 POTUS PORTRAYALS BROUGHT A RANGE OF ATTITUDES TO THE WHITE HOUSE

SERIOUS

PATRICIA WETTIG
as Caroline Reynolds
PRISON BREAK

ANTHONY HOPKINS
as Richard M. Nixon
NIXON

DANIEL DAY-LEWIS
as Abraham Lincoln
LINCOLN

PAUL GIAMATTI
as John Adams
JOHN ADAMS

JOSH BROLIN
as George W. Bush
W

MARTIN SHEEN
as Josiah "Jed" Bartlet
THE WEST WING

GREG KINNEAR
as John F. Kennedy
THE KENNEDYS

BILL PULLMAN
as Thomas J. Whitmore
INDEPENDENCE DAY

TONY GOLDWYN
as Fitzgerald "Fitz" Grant
SCANDAL

KEVIN SPACEY
as Francis Underwood
HOUSE OF CARDS

DENNIS HAYSBERT
as David Palmer
24

BILL MURRAY
as Franklin Delano Roosevelt
HYDE PARK ON HUDSON

MORGAN FREEMAN
as Tom Beck
DEEP IMPACT

HARRISON FORD
as James Marshall
AIR FORCE ONE

GEENA DAVIS
as Mackenzie Allen
COMMANDER IN CHIEF

DAN HEDAYA
as Richard M. Nixon
DICK

JULIA LOUIS-DREYFUS
as Selina Meyer
VEEP

JAMIE FOXX
as James Sawyer
WHITE HOUSE DOWN

CHRIS ROCK
as Mays Gilliam
HEAD OF STATE

KEVIN KLINE
as Bill Mitchell/Dave Kovic
DAVE

LLOYD BRIDGES
as Thomas "Tug" Benson
HOT SHOTS!

ROBIN WILLIAMS
as Teddy Roosevelt
THE NIGHT AT THE MUSEUM SERIES

JACK NICHOLSON
as James Dale
MARS ATTACKS!

JEFF BRIDGES
as Jackson Evans
THE CONTENDER

MICHAEL DOUGLAS
as Andrew Shepherd
THE AMERICAN PRESIDENT

HUMOROUS

BUMBLING

INSPIRING

11 Superman
Max and Dave Fleischer

In 1941, three years after the Man of Steel's first comic-book appearance, animator siblings Max and Dave Fleischer made a series of nine defining Superman shorts set in an art-deco cartoon world. They literally taught Superman how to fly—getting permission from DC, since in the comics he was just leaping tall buildings in a single bound.

THE FLASH

12 The Flash
Carmine Infantino

In a universe of brutes, monsters, and madmen, artist Infantino revitalized the Flash in 1956 as a lithe sprinter with the graceful calm of a marathon champ. Infantino (who died in 2013 at age 87) possessed a curlicue style that made the Flash a blurred ballet of red ribbons and knockout punches.

13 Phoenix
Chris Claremont and Dave Cockrum

Jean Grey lived up to her bland last name in the early X-Men tales until writer Chris Claremont and artist Dave Cockrum killed her and resurrected her as Phoenix in 1976. Possessed by a cosmic entity with sinister appetites, Grey went dark in the best way possible.

14 The Incredible Hulk
Bill Bixby and Lou Ferrigno

CONTINUES ON PAGE 82 ▶

THE BULLSEYE
Screen Couples

WE LOVED THEM. OR . . . NOT. HERE'S A LOOK AT THE SCREEN COUPLES THAT MADE US GO D'AWWW, AND SOME THAT MISSED THE MARK

1	ROSS AND RACHEL	Friends
2	MULDER AND SCULLY	The X-Files
3	COOKIE AND LUCIOUS	Empire
4	ALLIE AND NOAH	The Notebook
5	JESSE AND CELINE	Before Sunrise/Sunset/Midnight
6	JACK AND ROSE	Titanic
7	CARRIE AND BIG	Sex and the City
8	ENNIS DEL MAR AND JACK TWIST	Brokeback Mountain
9	MATTHEW AND MARY	Downton Abbey
10	JIM AND PAM	The Office
11	LUKE AND LORELAI	Gilmore Girls
12	OLIVIA AND FITZ	Scandal
13	BELLA AND EDWARD	the Twilight films
14	DEREK AND MEREDITH	Grey's Anatomy
15	BUFFY AND SPIKE	Buffy the Vampire Slayer
16	VIVIAN AND EDWARD	Pretty Woman
17	CHUCK AND SARAH	Chuck
18	HOMER AND MARGE	The Simpsons
19	BOOTH AND BONES	Bones
20	WILL AND VIOLA	Shakespeare in Love
21	CASTLE AND BECKETT	Castle
22	KURT AND BLAINE	Glee
23	JERRY AND DOROTHY	Jerry Maguire
24	LOGAN AND VERONICA	Veronica Mars
25	DAMON AND ELENA	Vampire Diaries

The lovers broke hearts around the world.

The perfect "will they or won't they?"

Cinderella in thigh-high pleather boots

Good for 50 shades of *Grey's*

Call them Caskett ("'cause of the whole murder thing").

Matthew and Mary, we hardly knew ye.

Hugh Jackman's body fat when he's in shape to play Wolverine

6%

From 1977 to '82, the tag team of Bill Bixby as David Banner and Lou Ferrigno as his raging alter ego on this TV series set the standard against which other Hulks have since been measured. We actually liked him a lot when he got angry.

15 Dream
Neil Gaiman

Introduced in 1989, this shadowy character from Gaiman's *Sandman* series is the immortal personification of fantasy. Known by many names, including simply Dream and Morpheus, he was the source of all stories, the forger of nightmares, and the worst boyfriend ever.

16 Wolverine
Hugh Jackman

From his muttonchops to his husky growl, Logan has always been all man, but Jackman's rock-solid take on the character in 2000's *X-Men* placed a big, beating heart inside that adaman-

tium metal rib cage. Wolverine proved so popular that he got his own spin-off movie in 2009, and a second in 2013.

17 Swamp Thing
Alan Moore

With these 1980s comics, Moore, a British writer, took a monstrous mound of sentient

WOLVERINE

bog moss and made him one of the most soulful, human, and—astoundingly—romantic characters in superhero fiction.

18 Hellboy
Mike Mignola

Artist-writer Mignola's demonic but lovable bruiser raised hell in heavenly ways when he debuted in the mid-'90s. At a time when good guys were turning bad in comic-book tales, Hellboy was a creature forged from evil, defying his nature to fight for what's right.

19 Oracle
John Ostrander and Kim Yale

The wildest thing about librarian Barbara Gordon's transformation from Batgirl into the wheelchair-bound Oracle wasn't that she was shot and paralyzed by the Joker. It was that writers Ostrander and Yale didn't try to erase that plot point when they brought her back in 1989 as an ever-watchful, hypernetworked hero-hacker. Oracle proved disability does not preclude power.

 THE INCREDIBLES

20 Astonishing X-Men
Joss Whedon

In 2004, fresh off his years in TV, Whedon moved on to Marvel's comic-book world of misfit mutants. His work was part off-the-cuff wit, part chaos, and part ethical and emotional quandary, presaging the panel-busting speed and scope he brought to the screen with 2012's *The Avengers*.

21 The Incredibles
Brad Bird

The 2004 Pixar film's premise of a family of superheroes living in dull suburbia, hiding their powers from the world, is brilliant in itself. But writer-director Bird added depth by fusing the superhero and spy-movie genres with dark comedy about midlife angst.

22 The Incredible Hulk
Stan Lee and Jack Kirby

Inspired by Dr. Jekyll and Mr. Hyde, Frankenstein, and A-bomb anxiety, writer Stan Lee and artist Jack Kirby introduced the Hulk in 1962 as a tragic, misunderstood monster whose internal conflict between responsibility and rage was as poignant as it was pulpy.

23 Star-Lord
Chris Pratt

As played with wily mischief by Chris Pratt in 2014's *Guardians of the Galaxy*, the swashbuckling interplanetary policeman also known as Peter Quill is like Han Solo's more excitable, less responsible nephew. Will he help his posse of merry misfits learn to overcome their selfishness? Of course he will.

24 Daredevil
Frank Miller

Miller's early-1980s twist on the blind lawyer–turned–street-fighting man rewrote the good guy's decades-long backstory and complemented Matt Murdock's sightlessness with newfound ruthlessness (and martial-arts skills).

25 Fantastic Four
Stan Lee and Jack Kirby

Starting in 1961, *Fantastic Four*—the ultimate expression of two very different flavors of comic-book genius—combined the cosmic vision of artist Jack Kirby with the bantering humanism of writer Stan Lee. The result was a superteam that was also a family unit, sparring with supervillains and one another. ■

FANTASTIC FOUR

Villains

FROM SERIAL KILLERS TO A WRITER'S NO. 1 FAN,
HERE ARE THE WORST (WHICH IS TO SAY, THE
BEST) OF THE BADDIES WE LOVED TO HATE

1 Hannibal Lecter

The Silence of the Lambs

He packs a lot of screams into only 25 minutes on screen. But that was long enough for Anthony Hopkins to nab an Oscar for his chillingly erudite cannibal in 1991's *The Silence of the Lambs*. MOST EVIL QUOTE: "A census taker once tried to test me. I ate his liver with some fava beans and a nice Chianti."

2 The Joker

Batman movies

Batman's greatest adversary is ruthlessly, functionally insane. As portrayed by Cesar Romero on TV, he's a little-j joker; played by Jack Nicholson on film, he's a violent hambone; in the hands of Heath Ledger, he's hair-raisingly awesome. MOST EVIL QUOTE: From *The Dark Knight*, "See, I'm not a monster—I'm just ahead of the curve."

"YOU LOOK
NERVOUS. IS IT
THE SCARS?"

3 Mr. Burns

The Simpsons

The Simpsons' 104-year-old billionaire, owner of the Springfield Nuclear Power Plant, boasts an insatiable appetite for wealth, power, and other people's unhappiness. MOST EVIL QUOTE: "Release the hounds!"

4 Voldemort

Harry Potter

Cruel with no hope of redemption, Harry Potter's nemesis (Ralph Fiennes in the films) is an old-school unrepentant, power-hungry, control freak. But his loathing for anyone who doesn't meet his definition of "normal" is utterly of the moment. MOST EVIL MOVE: Killing his own father.

5 Annie Wilkes

Misery

As *Misery*'s cheery psychopath who imprisons and tortures her favorite novelist, Paul Sheldon, for killing off her

number of puppies (plus 20 adult dogs) used in filming the live-action 101 Dalmatians **230**

favorite character, Kathy Bates is an unsettling mix of Squeaky Fromme and June Cleaver. MOST EVIL MOVE: Breaking both of Paul's ankles with a sledgehammer, then calmly saying, "God, I love you." (In Stephen King's original book, she chops off his foot with an ax.)

6 T-1000
Terminator 2: Judgment Day

Arnold Schwarzenegger's killing machine got sequelized into heroism, but Robert Patrick's protean assassin is his perfect match. A living-metal shape-changer with a

policeman's badge, he's a horror-movie creature and an avatar for the age of paranoia. MOST EVIL MOVE: Armblades.

7 Max Cady
Cape Fear

A lout in a Hawaiian shirt quoting Dante on a mission of dish-served-cold vengeance. He's a vision of psychopathy, but Robert De Niro also makes him dangerously compelling, cerebral and sensually unleashed. MOST EVIL MOVE: Flirting with his target's teenage daughter (Juliette Lewis, in her breakout role).

8 Cruella de Vil
101 Dalmatians

How do you out-cartoon a cartoon? It helps if you're Glenn Close, who transforms her fur fanatic into a high-fashion snob willing to do anything—even kill fivescore puppies—for the right look. She's like a G-rated Tony Montana. MOST EVIL MOVE: Did we mention how her big plan is to kill several dozen puppies and wear them as clothes?

9 Verbal Kint/ Keyser Söze
The Usual Suspects

The greatest trick the devil

CRUELLA DE VIL

ever pulled was convincing the world he didn't exist, and the greatest trick Kevin Spacey ever pulled was convincing the audience that he was playing a loser, not a criminal mastermind. MOST EVIL QUOTE: "And like that, he's gone."

10 Alonzo Harris
Training Day

From the moment Denzel Washington's corrupt cop force-feeds PCP to angelic Ethan Hawke, it's clear that Detective Harris crossed the line between good and evil a long time ago. MOST EVIL QUOTE: "King Kong ain't got s--- on me!"

11 Bane
The Dark Knight Rises

A terrorist, an anarchist, a counterrevolutionary, a philosophical zealot: Batman's masked nemesis is a compilation of several generations' worth of national-security concerns. Pretty buff, too. MOST EVIL MOVE: Cutting off Gotham

CONTINUES ON PAGE 86 ▶

GAME OF THRONES'
KING OF PAIN

stops believing in Magneto's capacity for good—despite all appearances to the contrary.

15 Agent Smith
The Matrix

There's something simultaneously corporate and federal about the Matrix's digital antibody—as if the Wolf of Wall Street joined the Secret Service. Hugo Weaving is an unflappable bespoke-suited badass: a program who hates his machine overlords almost as much as the humans he chases. MOST EVIL MOVE: Replicating himself across the entire digital world.

16 Sauron
The Lord of the Rings

Not just an evil person but Evil Itself, Sauron is less a tangible character than an omnipresent corruption threatening to turn anyone—even happy little hobbits—toward the darkness. MOST EVIL MOVE: His sole hobby is conquering all that has ever been and ever will be.

CONTINUES ON PAGE 88 ▶

from the mainland one bridge at a time.

12 William "Bill the Butcher" Cutting
Gangs of New York

Daniel Day-Lewis as Bill the Butcher—murderer, crime boss, friend to corrupt politicians, enemy to all immigrants—drapes himself in the American flag and remembers with special fondness the best man he ever killed. MOST EVIL

QUOTE: "I die a true American."

13 King Joffrey
Game of Thrones

A child of incest spoiled rotten by inhuman ambition, Joffrey Baratheon never learned what was right and drew tremendous pleasure from doing wrong. An excellent argument against helicopter parenting. MOST EVIL MOVE: Cutting off Ned Stark's head? That's bad. Right in front of his daughter?

That's bad. And the daughter is your bride-to-be? Dude. Chill.

14 Magneto
X-Men

Whether he's played by strapping young Michael Fassbender or a cagey elder Sir Ian McKellan, the militant mutant is a prime example of how every villain is a hero in his own mind. MOST EVIL MOVE: Every time he betrays Professor X, a friend who never

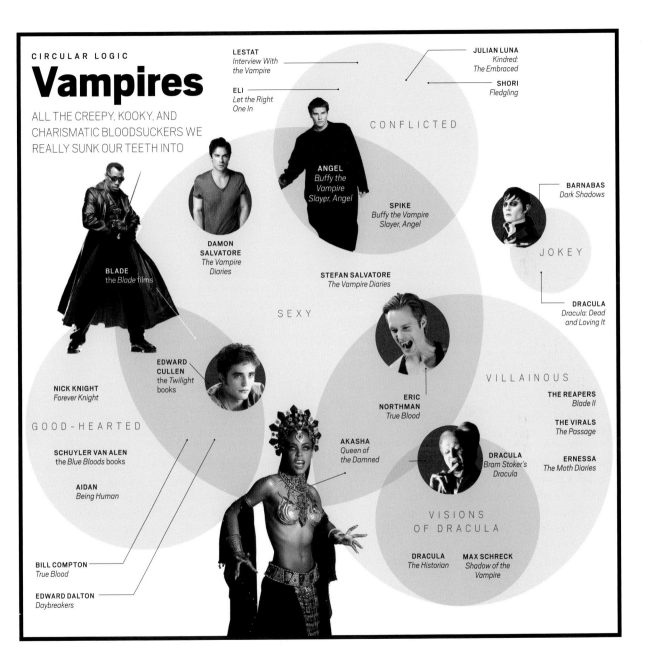

CIRCULAR LOGIC

Vampires

ALL THE CREEPY, KOOKY, AND
CHARISMATIC BLOODSUCKERS WE
REALLY SUNK OUR TEETH INTO

LESTAT
*Interview With
the Vampire*

JULIAN LUNA
*Kindred:
The Embraced*

SHORI
Fledgling

ELI
*Let the Right
One In*

CONFLICTED

ANGEL
*Buffy the
Vampire
Slayer, Angel*

SPIKE
*Buffy the Vampire
Slayer, Angel*

BARNABAS
Dark Shadows

JOKEY

**DAMON
SALVATORE**
*The Vampire
Diaries*

BLADE
the *Blade* films

STEFAN SALVATORE
The Vampire Diaries

DRACULA
*Dracula: Dead
and Loving It*

SEXY

**EDWARD
CULLEN**
the *Twilight*
books

**ERIC
NORTHMAN**
True Blood

VILLAINOUS

NICK KNIGHT
Forever Knight

THE REAPERS
Blade II

THE VIRALS
The Passage

GOOD-HEARTED

AKASHA
*Queen of
the Damned*

DRACULA
*Bram Stoker's
Dracula*

ERNESSA
The Moth Diaries

SCHUYLER VAN ALEN
the *Blue Bloods* books

AIDAN
Being Human

VISIONS
OF DRACULA

BILL COMPTON
True Blood

DRACULA
The Historian

MAX SCHRECK
*Shadow of the
Vampire*

EDWARD DALTON
Daybreakers

VILLAINS CONTINUED FROM PAGE 86

17 Hans Landa
Inglourious Basterds

Colonel Landa will talk your ear off in any language. (He knows them all.) As played by Christoph Waltz, Hans Landa is a delightfully inquisitive portrait of Nazi horror. Some call him the Jew hunter, but he's really a detective: Columbo for fascists. MOST EVIL QUOTE: "What's that American expression? 'If the shoe fits, you must wear it.'"

18 Edwin Epps
12 Years a Slave

Can you feel sympathy for the devil? A plantation owner in the slavery-era South, Epps (Michael Fassbender) is a monstrosity of a man: despotic, violent, drunk, a rapist who treats people like property. He is also a lonely, impotent little man.

MOST EVIL QUOTE: "I'll take the starch outta ya."

19 Scar
The Lion King

Really, though, wasn't Mufasa such a bore? And wasn't Simba such a little goody-two-shoes? The villains always get the best lines—ask Shakespeare—and this is as close as Disney's ever come to *Hamlet*. MOST EVIL MOVE: Killing his brother while his nephew watches in horror.

20 Anton Chigurh
No Country for Old Men

SCAR

An unstoppable force, an immovable object, and one hell of a bad haircut. Javier Bardem's supercriminal is a creature of myth, complete with an untraceable accent, beyond pain or petty notions of morality. MOST EVIL MOVE: He finds a creative new use for a cattle gun.

21 John Doe
Seven

The movie builds gradually to his first appearance. First he's a shadow, then, a myth. Finally, Kevin Spacey walks into a police station: bald, gentle, and covered in blood. *Seven*'s baddie is a uniquely meticulous madman—and Spacey's restraint makes him even more terrifying. MOST EVIL MOVE: Three words: Gwyneth Paltrow's head.

22 Patrick Bateman
American Psycho

Poor little Patrick just wants to be cool. Yes, he kills people. Yes, he's got a chainsaw in his closet and a couple of heads in his refrigerator. Can you blame him? It's stressful, the banking life. MOST EVIL LINE: "I like to dissect girls. Did you know I'm utterly insane?"

23 Doctor Evil
Austin Powers films

Step 1: Hijack some nuclear weapons. Step 2: Hold the world hostage. Step 3: Attach laser beams to the heads of killer sharks. Step 4: Make 1 million dollars. [cue evil laugh] MOST EVIL MOVE: From a managerial perspective, it's probably not a good idea to incinerate so many minions.

10

days the subway shootout between Agent Smith and Neo went over schedule

24 Mr. Blonde
Reservoir Dogs

The killer other killers worry about. After a heist goes wrong, Vic Vega smells a rat. The whole Tarantino era begins when Michael Madsen dances to "Stuck in the Middle With You"—right before he cuts off a captured cop's ear. MOST EVIL LINE: "All you can do is pray for a quick death, which you ain't gonna get."

25 The Borg Queen
Star Trek: First Contact

Star Trek's produced some memorable baddies over the years—"Khaaaaan!"—but Alice Krige's synthetic over-lord is the antagonist for the franchise's whole utopian idea. Brutally indifferent, she's the human impulse to explore negated into pure nihilism. MOST EVIL LINE: "Resistance is futile." ■

THE BORG QUEEN, *STAR TREK*

POP CULTURE OBSESSION

Zombies

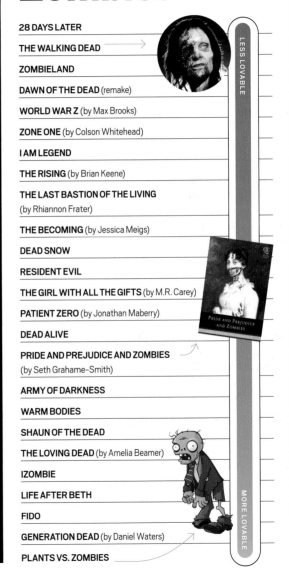

28 DAYS LATER

THE WALKING DEAD

ZOMBIELAND

DAWN OF THE DEAD (remake)

WORLD WAR Z (by Max Brooks)

ZONE ONE (by Colson Whitehead)

I AM LEGEND

THE RISING (by Brian Keene)

THE LAST BASTION OF THE LIVING (by Rhiannon Frater)

THE BECOMING (by Jessica Meigs)

DEAD SNOW

RESIDENT EVIL

THE GIRL WITH ALL THE GIFTS (by M.R. Carey)

PATIENT ZERO (by Jonathan Maberry)

DEAD ALIVE

PRIDE AND PREJUDICE AND ZOMBIES (by Seth Grahame-Smith)

ARMY OF DARKNESS

WARM BODIES

SHAUN OF THE DEAD

THE LOVING DEAD (by Amelia Beamer)

IZOMBIE

LIFE AFTER BETH

FIDO

GENERATION DEAD (by Daniel Waters)

PLANTS VS. ZOMBIES

LESS LOVABLE

MORE LOVABLE

Femmes Fatales

YOU CAN'T TAKE YOUR EYES OFF THEM—AND YOU'D BETTER NOT TURN YOUR BACK ON THEM. THESE DEVIOUS DAMES WILL HAUNT YOUR DREAMS

1. Catherine Tramell, *Basic Instinct* (Sharon Stone) A male fantasy transformed into a nightmare: a bisexual nymphomaniac who might sleep with or kill you.

2. Suzanne Stone Maretto, *To Die For* (Nicole Kidman) Blind ambition meets blonde ambition. Suzanne wants fame at any cost—and she's just delusional enough to get it.

3. Claire Underwood, *House of Cards* (Robin Wright) Behind every great man, there's a great woman. And behind every Machiavellian power-monger politician, there's a partner just as nefarious. (With better hair, too.)

4. Bridget Gregory, *The Last Seduction* (Linda Fiorentino) Beware a woman in trouble. Manipulative and brilliant, Bridget's a big New York City fish in a small-town pond.

5. Jane Smith, *Mr. and Mrs. Smith* (Angelina Jolie) An assassin hunting her assassin husband (Brad Pitt), who never stood a chance.

6. Nikita, *La Femme Nikita* (Peta Wilson) A wrongfully accused innocent forced into a world of double-crossing agents and crisscrossing alliances. Nikita's a tough trained superspy—and her greatest endurance challenge is how she holds onto her soul.

7. Meredith Johnson, *Disclosure* (Demi Moore) A lady boss who sexually harasses straight white men? Talk about leaning in! Meredith's a post-feminist cartoon, but Moore makes her an enthralling antagonist.

8. Amy Dunne, *Gone Girl* (Rosamund Pike) What happens when the perfect metropolitan New Yorker cool-girl goes domestic? Spoiler: You wouldn't like her when she's angry.

9. Selina Kyle, *Batman Returns* (Michelle Pfeiffer) Witness the healing powers of the psychotic break, as a shy lonely secretary gets reborn into a proud, unafraid, wild creature of the night.

10. Selina Kyle, *The Dark Knight Rises* (Anne Hathaway) The Catwoman legend reimagined for the Recessionary era, Hathaway's Selina Kyle is an amoral streetwise antihero searching for a new beginning—by any means necessary.

11. Mystique, the *X-Men* films (Rebecca Romijn) Covered in blue body paint, speaking only the bare minimum of dialogue, the model-turned-actress gave the shape-changing mutant balletic grace. She's Eastwood's Man With No Name with less clothes and fewer names.

12. Sil, *Species* (Natasha Henstridge)

She positively demands going all the way on the first date. In this case, "all the way" means "give birth immediately to an alien-human-hybrid monster."

13. Lara Croft, the *Lara Croft* movies (Angelina Jolie) Indiana Jones in skintight short shorts. Only Jolie could bring the bodacious videogame adventurer to life.

14. Gemma Teller Morrow, *Sons of Anarchy* (Katey Sagal) Lady Macbeth was a no-talent rookie compared to Queen Gemma. She'll do anything for her family—and anything to her family.

15. Ginger Knowles, *Swordfish* (Halle Berry) The perfect vehicle for Berry's sultry-sweet charisma, Ginger's less femme fatale than femme *mystérieuse*. That smirk could be deadly.

16. Lucinda Harris, *Derailed* (Jennifer Aniston) Successful, married, beautiful—and bored. Lucinda's a tantalizing siren for a man looking for excitement.

17. Kathryn Merteuil, *Cruel Intentions* (Sarah Michelle Gellar) Before *Mean Girls*, she was the meanest girl. Gellar's prep-school puppet master is villainous on a Biblical level. Literally: She keeps cocaine in her crucifix!

18. Cersei Lannister, *Game of Thrones* (Lena Headey) Men are such boys. Westeros needs a good, firm hand.

19. Xenia Onatopp, *GoldenEye* (Famke Janssen) A Soviet agent running rampant through the post-Cold War superspy private sector. James Bond's met so many women, but how many of them literally have killer thighs?

20. Samantha Caine/Charly Baltimore, *The Long Kiss Goodnight* (Geena Davis) An amnesiac small-town schoolteacher finds out she's got a mysterious espionage past. She's Jason Bourne for desperate housewives.

21. The Bride, *Kill Bill* (Uma Thurman) Left for dead on her wedding day—shot by her unborn baby's daddy!—the blood-splattered Bride awakes seeking vengeance. Just your average cowboy samurai assassin.

22. Sarah Walker, *Chuck* (Yvonne Strahovski) Every nerd's dream: a badass secret agent with a heart of gold. The central joke of *Chuck* is that the title should actually be *Sarah*.

23. Lynn Bracken, *L.A. Confidential* (Kim Basinger) A hooker cut to look like Veronica Lake, Lynn is the femme fatale gone meta: an alluring Hollywood dreamgirl who dreams of a regular old-fashioned normal life.

24. Saffron, *Firefly* (Christina Hendricks) An oft-married con lady with the power to seduce the whole solar system. A defining role for pre–*Mad Men* Hendricks, who plays Saffron like a chameleon. She's whatever you want—and you'll do whatever she desires.

25. Aeon Flux, *Aeon Flux* (Charlize Theron) Because every totalitarian postapocalyptic dystopia needs at least one gun-totin', jump-kickin', rebel acrobat.

Funniest People

THESE RULE BREAKERS AND JOKE MAKERS ARE
THE KINGS AND QUEENS OF MODERN COMEDY

1 Julia Louis-Dreyfus

An Emmy winner for three distinct roles: neurotic Elaine on *Seinfeld*, a single mom on *The New Adventures of Old Christine*, and a perpetually underestimated pol on *Veep*. MEMORABLE PUNCHLINE "I hate men, but I'm not a lesbian." (*Seinfeld*)

2 Chris Rock

In his searing stand-up act and in films like 2014's *Top Five*, Rock offers an astute, post-Richard Pryor take on race and gender relations. MEMORABLE PUNCHLINE "We got no wealthy black people....Shaq is rich. The guy who signs his check is wealthy."

3 Louis C.K.

He had been a journeyman comic's comic for years. But his semiautobiographical FX sitcom *Louie* catapulted him into being an unlikely star and voice for

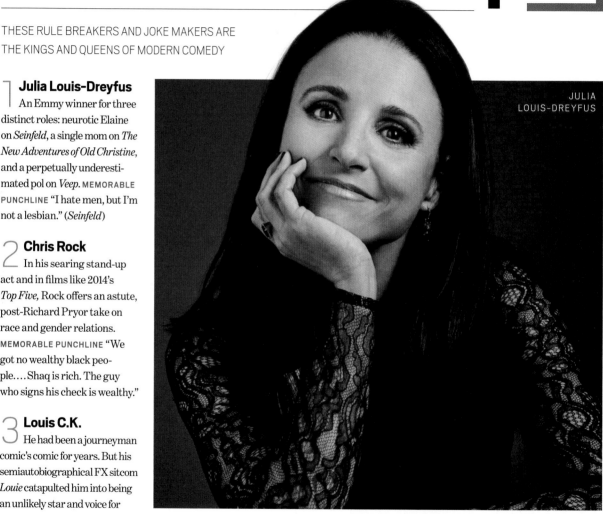

JULIA
LOUIS-DREYFUS

"I love being famous. It's almost like being white."

middle-aged schlubs everywhere. MEMORABLE PUNCHLINE "The meal isn't over when I'm full. It's over when I hate myself."

CHRIS ROCK

4 Tina Fey

As head writer of *SNL*, creator-star of *30 Rock*, and author of the best-seller *Bossypants*, she's equal parts cerebral and goofy. MEMORABLE PUNCHLINE "My ability to turn good news into anxiety is rivaled only by my ability to turn anxiety into chin acne."

5 Jerry Seinfeld

For nine seasons, he spun gold out of nothingness in one of the best sitcoms of all time, a pre-Internet meme machine (Soup Nazi, Master of My Domain, yadda yadda yadda). MEMORABLE PUNCHLINE "Boy, a little too much chlorine in that gene pool."

6 Amy Poehler

Who says comics have to be cynical? In seven years on *Saturday Night Live* and another seven on *Parks and Recreation*, she projected a sunny optimism that was refreshingly radical. MEMORABLE PUNCHLINE "Nothing is more depressing than a tired dominatrix."

LOUIS C.K.

CONTINUES ON PAGE 95 ▶

Best Comic-Relief Characters in Dramas

Louis Litt	SUITS
Lafayette Reynolds	TRUE BLOOD
The Dowager Countess	DOWNTON ABBEY
Castiel	SUPERNATURAL
Dorota Kishlovsky	GOSSIP GIRL
Stephen Holder	THE KILLING
Seth Cohen	THE O.C.
Odafin "Fin" Tutuola	LAW & ORDER: SVU
Saul Goodman	BREAKING BAD
Vince Masuka	DEXTER
Nolan Ross	REVENGE
Felicity Smoak	ARROW
Stiles Stilinski	TEEN WOLF
Paulie Walnuts	THE SOPRANOS
Bronn	GAME OF THRONES
Eli Gold	THE GOOD WIFE
Hoban "Wash" Washburne	FIREFLY
Felix Dawkins	ORPHAN BLACK
Chloe O'Brian	24
Sam Axe	BURN NOTICE
Dewey Crowe	JUSTIFIED
Hugo "Hurley" Reyes	LOST
Eddie Kessler	BOARDWALK EMPIRE
Mozzie	WHITE COLLAR
Data	STAR TREK: THE NEXT GENERATION

Jerry Seinfeld

DID'JA EVER NOTICE THAT THIS SUPREMELY TALENTED COMEDIAN CAN GET LAUGHS OUT OF LIFE'S MOST MUNDANE SITUATIONS?

180
EPISODES OF *SEINFELD* FILMED

380
entrances Kramer made on the show

43
comedians featured in six seasons of his web series *Comedians in Cars Getting Coffee*

9
number of seasons Jerry ended the show with, because the Beatles broke up after nine years and left him wanting more

five
EPISODES JERRY HAS NAMED AS HIS FAVORITES:

"The Boyfriend"
"The Contest"
"The Pothole"
"The Rye"
"The Yada Yada"

1998
year *Seinfeld* received an award from the American Academy of Dermatology, for the episode "The Slicer"

15
times Jerry says "Hello, Newman" throughout the series

2
times he's hosted *Saturday Night Live*

3
additional appearances on *SNL* (twice uncredited)

1
Seinfeld episode they tossed out shortly before filming because they didn't like it—it was about Jerry buying a handgun

68
EMMY NOMINATIONS

10
EMMY WINS

$820 MILLION+

HIS ESTIMATED NET WORTH

47
Porsches he reportedly owns

3
clips from his decades of TV stand-up performances he posts daily on jerryseinfeld .com

1981
year he first did stand-up on *The Tonight Show Starring Johnny Carson*

200
times he practiced his **5** minute set for the *Tonight Show*

0
number of Emmys Jerry won for acting

20
minutes a day he's said he spends doing Transcendental Meditation

$110 MILLION

AMOUNT NBC OFFERED JERRY TO DO A 10TH SEASON OF *SEINFELD*

$2.7 MILLION
box office gross of his 2002 documentary, *Comedian*

2.9 MILLION
Twitter followers

500+
new plotlines the Twitter page Modern Seinfeld (@seinfeldtoday) has devised for the "show about nothing"

$39.50 Cost of Kramer's Reality Tour of New York City, hosted by Kenny Kramer, inspiration for Michael Richards' character

CONTINUED FROM PAGE 93

7 Bill Murray

In movies like *Caddyshack*, *Ghostbusters* and *St. Vincent*, he made boorishness endearing. His best role? "Bill Murray," the Hollywood recluse who shuns handlers but photo-bombs strangers' weddings. **MEMORABLE PUNCHLINE** "Human sacrifice, dogs and cats living together…mass hysteria!" (*Ghostbusters*)

8 Melissa McCarthy

Her breakout role in *Bridesmaids* earned her an Oscar nod, and McCarthy emerged as a star with a gift for physical humor as well as brash, expletive-laden rants. **MEMORABLE PUNCHLINE** "I'm glad he's single, because I'm going to climb that like a tree." (*Bridesmaids*)

9 Eddie Murphy

Hollywood's first black global superstar has created some indelible characters: Gumby, Buckwheat, Axel Foley in *Beverly Hills Cop*, Donkey in *Shrek*, a whole family reunion's worth of Klumps in the *Nutty Professor* movies. **MEMORABLE PUNCHLINE** "Otay!"

10 Ricky Gervais

As co-creator and star of the BBC's original *The Office*, Gervais helped launch an era of mockumentaries as well as discomfiting social comedy. **MEMORABLE PUNCHLINE** "Some days you are the pigeon, and some days you are the statue."

11 Trey Parker and Matt Stone

The duo—buds since the University of Colorado, Boulder—relish making hamburger out of sacred cows, cunningly adopting innocuous forms like cut-paper animation (*South Park*) or marionettes (*Team*

CONTINUES ON PAGE 96 ▶

Yes, Tina Fey, we want you to go to there.

America: World Police).
FUNNIEST WORK 2011's Tony-
winning musical *The Book of
Mormon.*

12 Steve Carell
For the U.S. version of
The Office, Carell swapped the
casual cruelty of Ricky
Gervais' boss for an amiable
cluelessness. He's just as endearing in films like *The
40-Year-Old Virgin* and the
Despicable Me series. MEMORA-
BLE PUNCHLINE "That's what
she said."

13 Mindy Kaling
As an Indian-
American Dartmouth grad,
she's not your typical TV
star. But her characters on
The Office and *The Mindy
Project* were relatably universal. MEMORABLE PUNCHLINE
"There is no sunrise so beautiful that it is worth waking me
up to see it."

14 Kevin Hart
The pint-size power-
house may be the hardest-
working man in comedy,

TINA FEY

jumping from stand-up to
movie hits like *Ride Along* and
Think Like a Man. MEMORABLE
PUNCHLINE "I don't have exes.
I have Y's, like, 'Y the hell did
I date you?'"

15 Will Ferrell
Whether he's playing
George W. Bush or Buddy the
Elf or '70s anchordude Ron
Burgundy, Ferrell projects an
air of earnest befuddlement.
Even his jerks have charm.
MEMORABLE PUNCHLINE "I love
scotch. Scotchy scotch scotch."

16 Ben Stiller
The son of Jerry Stiller
and Anne Meara has comedy
in his blood. And he's proven it
as both a goofball (*Dodgeball*)
and put-upon straight man (the
Fockers movies). MEMORABLE
PUNCHLINE "I'm pretty sure
there's a lot more to life than
being really, really, ridiculously
good-looking?" (*Zoolander*)

CONTINUES ON PAGE 98 ▶

25 Memorable *SNL* Characters

SOME WE SAW RARELY, OTHERS A LOT; HOW FUNNY WERE THEY OVERALL?

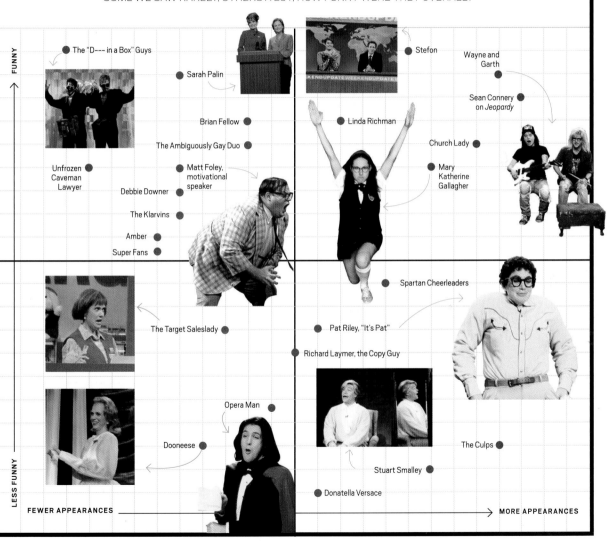

FUNNY

The "D--- in a Box" Guys

Stefon

Wayne and Garth

Sarah Palin

Sean Connery on *Jeopardy*

Brian Fellow

Linda Richman

The Ambiguously Gay Duo

Church Lady

Unfrozen Caveman Lawyer

Matt Foley, motivational speaker

Mary Katherine Gallagher

Debbie Downer

The Klarvins

Amber

Super Fans

Spartan Cheerleaders

The Target Saleslady

Pat Riley, "It's Pat"

Richard Laymer, the Copy Guy

Opera Man

Dooneese

The Culps

Stuart Smalley

Donatella Versace

LESS FUNNY

FEWER APPEARANCES

MORE APPEARANCES

KEY & PEELE

Wright's Three Flavours Cornetto trilogy, facing down zombies, criminals, and the apocalypse with everybloke aplomb. FUNNIEST WORK 2004's *Shaun of the Dead.*

19 David Sedaris

In his best-selling books, Sedaris brings his cockeyed sensibility to everything from his Southern upbringing to his early stint as an elf at Macy's Santaland. MEMORABLE PUNCHLINE "There's a reason regular people don't appear on TV: we're boring."

20 Amy Schumer

Her bawdy Comedy Central sketch show delivers spot-on parodies of Aaron Sorkin and *12 Angry Men*, but with a feminist slant. Her avatar in a *Call of Duty*-style videogame deals with rape and bureaucratic red tape. FUNNIEST WORK 2015's *Trainwreck.*

21 Bill Hader

The star of *Trainwreck*

and the *Cloudy With a Chance of Meatballs* films had a chameleonic eight-year run on *SNL*, playing Al Pacino, Vincent Price, and Manhattan's ultimate club kid Stefon. MEMORABLE PUNCHLINE "New York's hottest club is Heyyy!"

22 Lena Dunham

Dunham's tattooed, normal-size Hannah Horvath on *Girls* is a downtown millennial version of Carrie Bradshaw, similarly ambitious and just as clueless in romance. MEMORABLE PUNCHLINE "I can't wait to be 80. So I can shock people by saying 'rim job' in casual conversation."

23 Larry David

The co-creator of *Seinfeld* (and model for George Costanza) presented eight seasons of unchecked id on *Curb Your Enthusiasm*. MEMORABLE PUNCHLINE "Let me tell you something; I do hate myself, but it has nothing to do with being Jewish."

17 Key & Peele

The biracial Comedy Central stars have called themselves "black nerds"—not unlike Barack Obama, whom Peele plays in hilarious recurring sketches with Key as Luther, the buttoned-up president's "anger translator."

MEMORABLE PUNCHLINE "I said, 'Beeeeetch! I'm the man of the house.'"

18 Simon Pegg

Americans may know him as Scotty in the *Star Trek* reboots, but to Brits he's the lager-loving hero of Edgar

24 Abbi Jacobson & Ilana Glazer

Jacobson is the clumsy, straight-haired one; Glazer has a curly 'do and bizarre pronunciations ("Jah-net Jahx-son"). Together on *Broad City*, they're weed-loving twentysomethings flailing through dead-end jobs and relationships. MEMORABLE PUNCHLINE "Every animal from every movie we loved as a kid? Probably dead."

25 Bill Maher

The blunt, un-PC host of HBO's *Real Time with Bill Maher* is a modern Will Rogers for a generation exasperated by political hypocrisy, ambivalent about organized religion, and eager for legalized and easily obtainable weed. MEMORABLE PUNCHLINE "Atheism is a religion like abstinence is a sex position."∎

AMY SCHUMER

Belly-Busting *SNL* Sketches

	SKETCH	SEASON
1	"CHIPPENDALES AUDITIONS"	16
2	"MR. BELVEDERE FAN CLUB"	17
3	"MATT FOLEY, MOTIVATIONAL SPEAKER"	18
4	"THE DENISE SHOW"	19
5	"THE CHANUKAH SONG"	20
6	"THE ROXBURY GUYS"	21
7	"TOM BROKAW PRE-TAPES"	22
8	"DYSFUNCTIONAL FAMILY DINNER"	23
9	"NPR'S 'DELICIOUS DISH:' SCHWEDDY BALLS"	24
10	"BEHIND THE MUSIC: BLUE ÖYSTER CULT"	25
11	"FIRST PRESIDENTIAL DEBATE"	26
12	"PATRIOTIC SHORTS"	27
13	"COLONEL ANGUS"	28
14	"DEBBIE DOWNER"	29
15	"WOOMBA"	30
16	"LAZY SUNDAY"	31
17	"D--- IN A BOX"	32
18	"GOOGLY EYES GARDENER"	33
19	"SARAH PALIN AND HILLARY CLINTON ADDRESS THE NATION"	34
20	"CENSUS TAKER"	35
21	"WHAT'S THAT NAME?"	36
22	"MAYA ANGELOU'S I KNOW WHY THE CAGED BIRD LAUGHS!"	37
23	"STEFON'S HALLOWEEN TIPS"	38
24	"(DO IT ON MY) TWIN BED"	39
25	"BLACK WIDOW TRAILER"	40

Spies

WE CAN'T GET ENOUGH OF
INTERNATIONAL ESPIONAGE. TAKE
A TRIP AROUND THE WORLD TO
THESE SPIES' SECRET (AND NOT-SO-
SECRET) HIDEOUTS.

NEW YORK CITY

5. Sterling Archer, **ARCHER**
6. Michael Wiseman, **NOW AND AGAIN**

LONDON

18. James Bond, **SKYFALL**
19. George Smiley, **TINKER TAILOR SOLDIER SPY**
20. Austin Powers, **THE AUSTIN P SERIES**
21. Galahad, **KINGSMAN: THE SE SERVICE**

WASHINGTON

7. Annie Walker, **COVERT AFFAIRS**
8. Rowan Pope, **SCANDAL**
9. Elizabeth and Philip Jennings, **THE AMERICANS** (see also Russia)
10. Susan Cooper, **SPY**
11. Evelyn Salt, **SALT** (see also Russia)
12. Jack Ryan, **THE TOM CLANCY BOOKS**

CALIFORNIA

1. Jack Bauer, **24**
2. Maxwell Smart, **GET SMART**
3. Sydney Bristow, **ALIAS**
4. Chuck Bartowski, **CHUCK**

EUROPE

13. Jason Bourne, **THE BOURNE SERIES**
14. Ethan Hunt, **THE MISSION: IMPOSSIBLE SERIES**
15. Napoleon Solo, **THE MAN FROM U.N.C.L.E.**
16. Nikita, **LA FEMME NIKITA**

EAST GERMANY

17. Hauptmann Gerd Wiesler of the Stasi, **THE LIVES OF OTHERS**

RUSSIA

9. Elizabeth and Philip Jennings, **THE AMERICANS**
11. Evelyn Salt, **SALT**

MIDDLE EAST

22. Carrie Mathison, **HOMELAND**
23. Maya, **ZERO DARK THIRTY**
24. Tony Mendez, **ARGO**

ISRAEL

25. Gabriel Allon, **THE DANIEL SILVA BOOKS**

Transformations

WHEN THESE STARS METAMORPHOSED FOR MAJOR ROLES, THEY WOWED AUDIENCES—AND COURTED AWARDS

NICOLE KIDMAN
IN *THE HOURS*

1 Nicole Kidman
The Hours (2002)

To play the poet Virginia Woolf, the Oscar winner donned a wig and a beak-like prosthetic nose that obscured her familiar face. Added bonus: "The paparazzi would be outside my trailer," she told *EW* at the time, "and they'd have no idea it was me."

2 Steve Carell
Foxcatcher (2014)

The rubber-faced comic actor wore aging makeup and a fake nose as well as a close-cropped graying hairstyle to portray murderous pharma heir John du Pont. Then he flattened his voice to an affectless burr.

3 Charlize Theron
Monster (2003)

How does a former model earn cred as an actress (and an Academy Award)? By uglifying herself with prosthetic teeth and a 30-pound weight gain in a film about real-life female serial killer Aileen Wournos.

4 Christian Bale
The Machinist (2004)

Bale, who's ordinarily 6'2" and 180 pounds, dropped to a skeletal 120 pounds on a daily diet of water, an apple, and a cup of coffee. He also slept for just two hours a night to better look like the insomniac hero.

5 George Clooney
Syriana (2005)

Defying the emaciating trend of many actors, Clooney actually gained 30 pounds (and grew a beard) for his Oscar-winning performance in Stephen Gaghan's fact-based thriller.

6 Hilary Swank
Boys Don't Cry (1999)

Before production began on the film about Brandon Teena, a transgender guy in 1990s

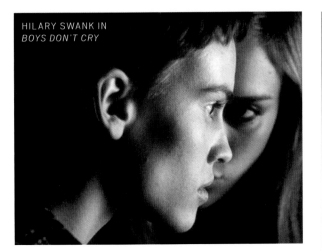

HILARY SWANK IN
BOYS DON'T CRY

Nebraska, Swank bound her breasts and attempted to live for four weeks as a man.

7 Jennifer Aniston
Cake (2014)

In a big-screen make-under that earned her a Golden Globe nod, the former *Friends* star shunned most makeup, scarred her cheek, and donned drawstring pants to play a woman sidelined by chronic pain.

8 Matthew McConaughey
Dallas Buyers Club (2013)

As a Southern good ol' boy who contracts HIV in the 1980s, the Texas-born McConaughey lost more than 40 pounds. But he picked up his first Oscar

for his troubles.

9 Jared Leto
Dallas Buyers Club (2013)

McConaughey's costar also lost 30 pounds for the film, but his Oscar-winning transformation began with his wig-to-heels embodiment of HIV-positive transsexual Rayon—the actor even stayed in character when the cameras were off.

10 Renée Zellweger
Bridget Jones' Diary (2001)

The petite 31-year-old Texas native bulked up 25 pounds to play the weight-obsessed

CONTINUES ON PAGE 106 ▶

Screen Smarts

BRANIACS OR BOZOS, THEY'RE ALL BIG PERSONALITIES

	GENIUS ... DIMWIT	
Stephen Hawking		THE THEORY OF EVERYTHING
John Nash		A BEAUTIFUL MIND
Dr. Gregory House		HOUSE
Sherlock Holmes		SHERLOCK
Finch		PERSON OF INTEREST
Will Hunting		GOOD WILL HUNTING
Sheldon Cooper		THE BIG BANG THEORY
Data		STAR TREK: THE NEXT GENERATION
Temperance "Bones" Brennan		BONES
Tony Stark		IRON MAN
Adrian Monk		MONK
Chris Gardner		THE PURSUIT OF HAPPYNESS
Hermione Granger		THE HARRY POTTER FILMS
Mike Ross		SUITS
Lisa Simpson		THE SIMPSONS
Joey Tribbiani		FRIENDS
Jar Jar Binks		THE STAR WARS PREQUELS
Brittany Pierce		GLEE
Bubble		ABSOLUTELY FABULOUS
Butt-Head		BEAVIS AND BUTT-HEAD
Harry and Lloyd		DUMB & DUMBER
Derek Zoolander		ZOOLANDER
Kevin Malone		THE OFFICE
Patrick Star		SPONGEBOB SQUAREPANTS
Brick Tamland		THE ANCHORMAN FILMS

Detectives

SOME TAPPED OUR FUNNY BONES, OTHERS TOUCHED OUR HEARTS.
BUT THEY ALL HAD US WAITING FOR WHAT CAME NEXT

WORKING THEIR QUIRKS

1	Ace Ventura	ACE VENTURA: PET DETECTIVE	8	Brenda Leigh Johnson	THE CLOSER
2	Frank Drebin	THE NAKED GUN FILMS	9	Patrick Jane	THE MENTALIST
3	Adrian Monk	MONK	10	Hercule Poirot	HERCULE POIROT
4	Shawn Spencer and Burton "Gus" Guster	PSYCH	11	Ezekiel "Easy" Rawlins	THE WALTER MOSLEY BOOKS
5	Claire DeWitt	THE SARA GRAN BOOKS	12	Veronica Mars	VERONICA MARS
6	Richard Castle and Kate Beckett	CASTLE	13	John Rebus	THE IAN RANKIN BOOKS
7	Martin Riggs and Roger Murtaugh	THE LETHAL WEAPON FILMS			

ALL BUSINESS

TRANSFORMATIONS CONTINUED FROM PAGE 103

London singleton from Helen Fielding's best-seller, but the heftier challenge: mastering a British accent.

11 Jake Gyllenhaal
Nightcrawler (2014)

The actor switched to a diet of kale and chewing gum to give an added sense of hunger to the creepy paparazzo Leo Bloom. He even ran 15 miles each night from his L.A. home to the film's set.

THE INFORMANT

12 Jake Gyllenhaal
Prince of Persia: The Sands of Time (2010)

Gyllenhaal reportedly worked out three times a day, six days a week to bulk up for the video-game-inspired flick.

13 Rooney Mara
The Girl With the Dragon Tattoo (2011)

Goth hacker Lisbeth Salander was a huge departure for the well-bred granddaughter of the New York Giants' owner. Mara even had her lip, brow, nose, and nipples pierced for the role.

14 Matt Damon
Courage Under Fire (1996)

For his breakout role as a heroin-addicted Gulf War veteran, the young actor lost a shocking 40 pounds by sticking to a strict diet and training regimen that threw off his metabolism for years.

15 Matt Damon
The Informant (2009)

The actor gained 30 pounds and grew a wispy mustache to play a frumpy biochemist

CONTINUES ON PAGE 109 ▶

Mobsters

HERE'S A LOOK AT THE WISEGUYS THAT WERE RIGHT ON TARGET—AND SOME THAT MISSED THE MARK

1	Tony Soprano (James Gandolfini)	THE SOPRANOS
2	Gustavo "Gus" Fring (Giancarlo Esposito)	BREAKING BAD
3	Enoch "Nucky" Thompson (Steve Buscemi)	BOARDWALK EMPIRE
4	Paul Vitti (Robert De Niro)	ANALYZE THIS
5	Lau Kin Ming (Andy Lau)	INFERNAL AFFAIRS
6	Vincent Vega (John Travolta)	PULP FICTION
7	William "Bill the Butcher" Cutting (Daniel Day-Lewis)	GANGS OF NEW YORK
8	John Dillinger (Johnny Depp)	PUBLIC ENEMIES
9	Fat Tony	THE SIMPSONS
10	Keyser Söze (Kevin Spacey)	THE USUAL SUSPECTS
11	Tommy DeVito (Joe Pesci)	GOODFELLAS
12	Frank Costello (Jack Nicholson)	THE DEPARTED
13	Frank Lucas (Denzel Washington)	AMERICAN GANGSTER
14	Nikolai Luzhin (Viggo Mortensen)	EASTERN PROMISES
15	Stringer Bell (Idris Elba)	THE WIRE
16	Sonny LoSpecchio (Chazz Palminteri)	A BRONX TALE
17	Michael Sullivan Sr. (Tom Hanks)	ROAD TO PERDITION
18	Bugsy Siegel (Warren Beatty)	BUGSY
19	Ellsworth "Bumpy" Johnson (Laurence Fishburne)	HOODLUM
20	Sam "Ace" Rothstein (Robert De Niro)	CASINO
21	Cheech (Chazz Palminteri)	BULLETS OVER BROADWAY
22	Carlito Brigante (Al Pacino)	CARLITO'S WAY
23	Frank Falenczyk (Ben Kingsley)	YOU KILL ME
24	Benjamin "Lefty" Ruggiero (Al Pacino)	DONNIE BRASCO
25	Ray "Bones" Barboni (Dennis Farina)	GET SHORTY

The Zen master of crime.

Tony, we miss your conflicted Mob-
boss ways—and the man who
brought you to life even more.

The beating,
bloody heart of one
of *Pulp Fiction*.

What happens in
Vegas stays in
Vegas, except for
what happened to
real-life gangster
Bugsy.

De Niro's comic riff
had us shrink-rapt.

Anna Paquin

AS A CHILD, SHE EARNED THE MOVIES' HIGHEST HONOR, THEN SHE TRIUMPHED AS TWO OF FANTASY'S MOST BADASS WOMEN

one
role she had prior to *The Piano*: playing a skunk

11
age when she won the Best Supporting Actress Oscar for *The Piano* in 1994 (the second-youngest person ever to win, after 10-year-old Tatum O'Neal)

20
seconds she was speechless at the podium when she accepted her award (Google it!)

5,000
other girls who auditioned for her part in *The Piano*

13
her age when she moved from New Zealand to Hollywood with her mother to pursue acting

19
her age when she made her stage debut, in *The Glory of Living* Off-Broadway

1
year she studied at Columbia University, before leaving to pursue her acting

150,000
Twitter followers

$10,000
amount *Late Show with David Letterman* donated in her name to charity after she sank a basketball shot on-air in 1996

80

geese that were trained for *Fly Away Home*; they were played voice recordings of Anna's voice before she arrived on set

1
Emmy nomination (for *Bury My Heart at Wounded Knee*)

1
Golden Globe award win (for *True Blood*)

14 MILLION

HER ESTIMATED NET WORTH

one
porn parody of *True Blood* (Anna and her costar/husband Stephen Moyer gave it out as a crew gift one year)

80
episodes of *True Blood* she did

$275,000
amount she was making per episode by 2013

0
vampire movies she saw before taking her role in *True Blood*

1
video Snoop Dogg has made, "Oh Sookie," about his love of Anna's *True Blood* character, Sookie Stackhouse

2010
year she came out as bisexual in a PSA supporting LGBT equality

year Sookie became the fastest-rising new name for baby girls

4
X-Men movies in which she's played Rogue

1
change she'd like to see for her *X-Men* character if she plays her again: Rogue should get to fly, as she does in the comics

2
films in which she costarred with Jeff Daniels: 1996's *Fly Away Home*, where she played his daughter, and 2005's *The Squid and the Whale*, where she played his girlfriend

1
pair of fraternal twins she gave birth to in 2012 (dad is her husband, Stephen Moyer)

1
film she produced with her husband through their production company, CASM Films: 2013's *Free Ride*

CONTINUED FROM PAGE 106

who blows the whistle on his company's price-fixing schemes to the FBI.

16 Anne Hathaway
Les Misérables (2012)
After bulking up to play Catwoman in *The Dark Knight Rises,* the actress shed 25 pounds on a restrictive diet of two daily squares of oatmeal paste to embody single mom-turned-prostitute Fantine. The prize for her acting-trumps-singing approach: an Oscar.

17 Linda Hamilton
Terminator 2: Judgment Day (1991)
To reprise her role as Sarah Connor, the 5-foot-6-inch actress went Schwarzenegger on her body, training three hours a day (she could bench-press 85 pounds) and eating a nonfat diet that helped her lose 12 pounds.

18 Demi Moore
G.I. Jane (1997)
Did I shave my head for this? Cast as the first female Navy SEAL, Moore not only clipped her signature brunette locks, she underwent intense military-style training to get into buff, fighting shape—and do all those one-handed push-ups.

19 Tom Hanks
Cast Away (2000)
Director Robert Zemeckis halted production for

CONTINUES ON PAGE 110 ▶

TRANSFORMATIONS CONTINUED FROM PAGE 109

TOM HANKS IN
CAST AWAY

nearly a year so Hanks could drop from his bulked-up 225 pounds to 170 and grow out his caveman-like beard as a guy stranded on a remote island. His one indulgence? Coffee.

20 Brad Pitt
Troy (2004)

To pack on 10 pounds of brawn for the Greek hero Achilles, Pitt reportedly endured months of two-to-three-hour gym sessions, plus an additional two hours of

sword training each day. Oh, and four high-protein, low-carb meals.

21 Robin Williams
Mrs. Doubtfire (1993)

It took more than just cake frosting to transform Williams into the aged Scottish nanny. Oscar-winner makeup artist Ve Neill spent four hours each day applying a multipart facial mask and then painting it to complete the look.

GUARDIANS OF
THE GALAXY

22 Chris Pratt
Guardians of the Galaxy (2014)

He's the chubby dude from *Parks and Rec* no more. After climbing to nearly 300 pounds for the comedy *Delivery Man*, Pratt dropped 60 pounds and got into beefy, ab-tastic shape as Star-Lord Peter Quill.

23 Michael Fassbender
Hunger (2008)

The already wiry actor turned into a walking ghost by starving himself to lose 30 pounds in 10 weeks—all to play a real-life Irish activist who launches a hunger strike to protest British prison conditions.

24 Meryl Streep
Into the Woods (2014)

Streep stooped her posture and lifted one shoulder to play the Witch—but she also got an assist with a bark-like black dress, a scraggly gray wig, crooked teeth inserts, and a prosthetic forehead and chin.

25 Domhnall Gleeson
Unbroken (2014)

The 32-year-old actor expected his role as an American prisoner of war in World War II-era Japan would be uncomfortable. But he reportedly became so dehydrated that his contact lenses didn't fit anymore. ∎

Child Actors

THESE TINY SUPERSTARS MESMERIZED
US AND WON OUR HEARTS

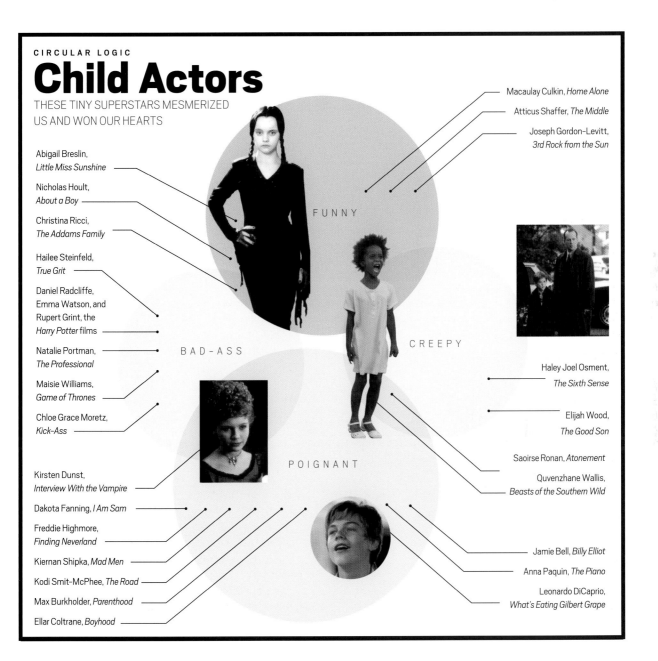

Abigail Breslin,
Little Miss Sunshine

Nicholas Hoult,
About a Boy

Christina Ricci,
The Addams Family

Hailee Steinfeld,
True Grit

Daniel Radcliffe,
Emma Watson, and
Rupert Grint, the
Harry Potter films

Natalie Portman,
The Professional

Maisie Williams,
Game of Thrones

Chloe Grace Moretz,
Kick-Ass

Kirsten Dunst,
Interview With the Vampire

Dakota Fanning, *I Am Sam*

Freddie Highmore,
Finding Neverland

Kiernan Shipka, *Mad Men*

Kodi Smit-McPhee, *The Road*

Max Burkholder, *Parenthood*

Ellar Coltrane, *Boyhood*

FUNNY

BAD-ASS

CREEPY

POIGNANT

Macaulay Culkin, *Home Alone*

Atticus Shaffer, *The Middle*

Joseph Gordon-Levitt,
3rd Rock from the Sun

Haley Joel Osment,
The Sixth Sense

Elijah Wood,
The Good Son

Saoirse Ronan, *Atonement*

Quvenzhane Wallis,
Beasts of the Southern Wild

Jamie Bell, *Billy Elliot*

Anna Paquin, *The Piano*

Leonardo DiCaprio,
What's Eating Gilbert Grape

Animation

THEY MAY BE ANIMATED, BUT THEY HAVE A SOUL. THESE 25 WERE DRAWN TO MAKE US LAUGH AND CRY

BEAUTY AND THE BEAST

1 The Beast
Beauty and the Beast (1991)
For his arrogance, he's cursed with a beastly body and a bison's head until he falls for a bookworm named Belle, whose love breaks the spell.

2 Simba
The Lion King (1994)
It's a Disney cartoon, so of course the lion-cub protagonist has no mother. But he is voiced by then-*Home Improvement* pinup Jonathan Taylor Thomas.

3 Vanellope von Schweetz

Wreck-It Ralph (2012)
Videogame glitches have never been as charming as Sarah Silverman's malfunctioning go-kart racer in a candy-striped racing game called Sugar Rush.

4 SpongeBob

SpongeBob Squarepants (1999-)
Bob may only be a deep-sea sponge with a job as a fry cook and the voice of a Munchkin, but he has enthusiasm to spare.

5 Princess Mononoke

Princess Mononoke (1997)
In Hayao Miyazaki's epic anime classic, San is a nature-loving human who's been raised by wolves and seeks to preserve the forest spirit.

6 Baymax

Big Hero 6 (2014)
Built soft and squishy like a giant Stay Puft marshmallow, this health-care robot transforms into a heroic fighter.

7 Dora

Dora the Explorer (2000-)
With Boots the monkey by her side, this purple-backpack-wearing Latina adventurer is the go-to detective for stolen goods.

8 Elsa

Frozen (2013)
Though it was purely accidental when she injured her sister with her magic ice-making powers, this banished princess just can't let it go.

PRINCESS MONONOKE

CONTINUES ON PAGE 114 ▶

Bonus!

Best Performances by Animals

- **The Dog**, played by Uggie the Jack Russell terrier, *The Artist*
- **Mr. Bigglesworth**, played by the hairless Sphynx SGC Belfry Ted Nude-Gent, the *Austin Powers* films
- **Bruiser Woods**, played by Chico the Chihuahua, the *Legally Blonde* films
- **Monkey**, played by Crystal the capuchin monkey, *The Hangover Part II*
- **Eddie**, played by Moose the Jack Russell terrier, *Frasier*
- **Frank the Pug**, played by Mushu the pug, the *Men in Black* films
- **Willy**, played by Keiko the orca whale, *Free Willy*
- **Beethoven**, played by Chris the Saint Bernard, the *Beethoven* films
- **The bear**, played by Bart the Alaskan Kodiak bear, *The Edge*
- **Air Buddy**, played by Buddy the golden retriever, the *Air Bud* films
- **Winter** the bottle-nosed dolphin, played by herself, *Dolphin Tale*
- **Skip**, played by Enzo the Jack Russell terrier, *My Dog Skip*
- **Joey**, played by multiple horses including Finder, *War Horse*
- **Murray**, played by the collie mix Maui, *Mad About You*
- **Grumpy Cat**, Internet celeb and star of *Grumpy Cat's Worst Christmas Ever*
- **Bear**, played by Graubaer's Boker, a Belgian Malinois, *Person of Interest*
- **Babe**, played a white Yorkshire pig, *Babe*
- **Gidget**, the Taco Bell Chihuahua
- **Hachi**, played by three Akitas, Chico, Layla, and Forrest, *Hachi*
- **The Burmese python**, played by Kitty, *Snakes on a Plane*
- **Seabiscuit**, played by several horses including Popcorn Deelites, *Seabiscuit*
- **Jack**, played by Chiquita and Pablo the capuchin monkeys, the *Pirates of the Caribbean* movies
- **Athansor** the magical horse, played by Listo, *Winter's Tale*
- **Archie**, played by Tank the Bear, *Dr. Doolittle 2*
- **Cashew**, played by three guinea pigs, but mostly Oscar, *House of Cards*

ANIMATION CONTINUED FROM PAGE 113

9 Olaf
Frozen (2013)
The antic snowman in *Frozen*'s wintry wonderland (voiced by Josh Gad) has a paradoxical affection for all things summery.

10 Dug
Up (2009)
Thanks to a high-tech device in his collar, this sweet, easily distracted golden retriever can communicate his thoughts ("Squirrel!") with humans.

11 Edna Mode
The Incredibles (2004)
Dahling, this diminutive half-Japanese, half-German force of nature is like a combo of Hollywood costumer Edith Head and Q from the Bond films.

12 Sheriff Woody
the *Toy Story* films (1995-)
Tom Hanks gives just the right laconic gentility to a Western hero so old-fashioned he fears kids may have moved on to flashier toys.

13 Buzz Lightyear
the *Toy Story* films (1995-)
At first, Tim Allen's battery-powered astronaut seemed vain but invincible. But over time (and two sequels), Buzz shows vulnerability as he realizes he can't remain the new-new thing forever.

"NO CAPES."

BUZZ-ING AROUND

14 Shrek
the *Shrek* films (2001–)
He can be a bit ogre-bearing, but the plus-size green giant has a gentle heart.

15 Merida
Brave (2012)
With her unruly shock of red hair and tomboyish ways, the Scottish heroine takes a bow and arrow to the typical Disney-princess stereotypes.

16 Stitch
Lilo and Stitch (2002)
The result of an illegal genetic experiment, the rambunctious Stitch poses as a dog and gets adopted by an Elvis-loving Hawaiian girl named Lilo.

17 Dory
Finding Nemo (2003)
Stranded little Nemo's hilariously ditzy sidekick is a blowfish who can't remember Hootie—or anything for more than five seconds.

18 Toothless
the *How to Train Your Dragon* films (2010-)
A fearsome Night Fury dragon with retractable teeth and a prosthetic tail fin courtesy of his teenage Viking buddy Hiccup.

19 **The Minions**
the *Despicable Me* films (2010-)
The Big Bird-yellow, capsule-shaped henchmen of super-villain Gru are loyal but impulsive, like untrained puppies.

20 **The Genie**
Aladdin (1992)
The late Robin Williams delivered one of his most riff-heavy, caffeinated performances as the Disney cartoon's genie. Ah, there's the rub.

21 **Coraline**
Coraline (2009)
An adventurous 11-year-old who discovers a portal to the fantastical Other World, complete with spooky alternate versions of her parents and neighbors.

22 **Jack Skellington**
The Nightmare Before Christmas (1993)
In Tim Burton's stop-motion fantasy world, he's the skeleton-like Pumpkin King of Halloween Town with a ghost dog named Zero for a pet.

23 **LEGO Batman**
The LEGO Movie (2014)
Will Arnett's version of the DC superhero is an egotistical jerk and boyfriend of the tech-savvy Wyldstyle; he's primed to get his own spin-off movie in 2017.

24 **Sterling Malory Archer**
Archer (2009-)
The self-centered, Kenny Loggins-loving superspy seems drawn to espionage mostly for its trappings—the women, cars, gadgets, and turtleneck sweaters.

25 **Kenny McCormick**
South Park (1997-)
The perpetually short-lived elementary schooler delivers his typically profane lines in a mumble, thanks to the parka covering his mouth. Then he dies. ∎

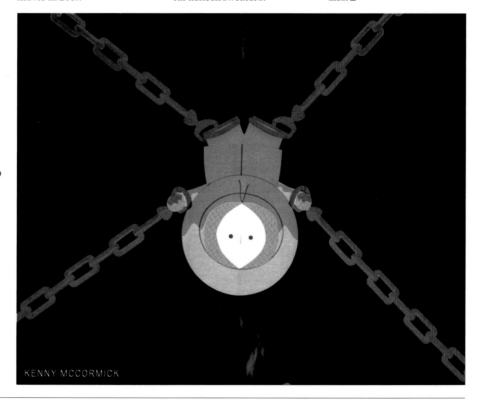

KENNY McCORMICK

3

Story Elements

From groundbreaking moments in screen steam and special effects to the most memorable dysfunctional families, dystopian worlds, and on-screen demises, these are the plot twists and story elements that made for unforgettable entertainment. Plus: our picks for the unsexiest sex scenes, best late night comedy bits, and weirdest weddings.

Steamiest MOMENTS

IT'S GETTING HOT IN HERE—AS WE PAY TRIBUTE TO THE BEST IN 25 YEARS OF THE SCREEN'S HOTTEST SCENES

OUT OF SIGHT

1 Out of Sight
1998

When George Clooney's bank robber and Jennifer Lopez's U.S. Marshal squeeze into the trunk of a car, they intimately spoon with a red-hot sensuality that surprises both of them (and us). It's a meet-cute in a unique setting and one of the most erotically charged moments of modern movies.

2 Mr. & Mrs. Smith
2005

The power couple as action heroes: Brad Pitt and Angelina Jolie made a movie about John and Jane, married assassins who must take each other out with really big guns, which ends up turning them on—on screen and in real life, as it happened. Angry, aroused, and armed to the teeth, they hit the dance floor to surreptitiously pat each other down. Quips hubby to his touchy-feely wife: "That's all John, sweetheart."

3 Buffy the Vampire Slayer
season 6, 2001

There's plenty of heat surrounding our blond heroine and her vampire beaux Angel and Spike—but all that biting and fighting and soul-losing kind of kills the buzz. What turns us on is the floaty joy of Tara (Amber Benson) and Willow (Alyson Hannigan), which reached glorious (literal) heights during the musical episode "Once More, With Feeling."

MR. & MRS. SMITH

Memorable Rom-Com Boyfriends

SEXY OR SILLY, THESE GUYS WERE ALL CRUSHABLE

George Clooney	DIVINE	ONE FINE DAY
John Corbett		MY BIG FAT GREEK WEDDING
Matthew McConaughey		HOW TO LOSE A GUY IN 10 DAYS
Ben Chaplin		THE TRUTH ABOUT CATS & DOGS
Michael Ealy		THINK LIKE A MAN
Jude Law		THE HOLIDAY
Taye Diggs		BROWN SUGAR
Heath Ledger		10 THINGS I HATE ABOUT YOU
Richard Gere		PRETTY WOMAN
Josh Lucas		SWEET HOME ALABAMA
Larenz Tate		LOVE JONES
Tom Hanks		YOU'VE GOT MAIL
Bill Pullman		WHILE YOU WERE SLEEPING
Colin Firth		BRIDGET JONES'S DIARY
Mark Ruffalo		13 GOING ON 30
Jack Nicholson		SOMETHING'S GOTTA GIVE
Michael Cera		NICK & NORAH'S INFINITE PLAYLIST
LL Cool J		DELIVER US FROM EVA
Hugh Grant		NOTTING HILL
Bradley Cooper		SILVER LININGS PLAYBOOK
Joseph Gordon-Levitt		500 DAYS OF SUMMER
Johnny Depp		BENNY & JOON
Adam Sandler	DORKY	THE WEDDING SINGER
Ryan Gosling		LARS AND THE REAL GIRL
Steve Carell		THE 40-YEAR-OLD VIRGIN

4 Alias
season 2, 2003

The opening moments of "Phase One"—in which Sydney Bristow (Jennifer Garner) vamps in spectacular underwear as AC/DC's "Back in Black" blares—perfectly encapsulate this spy show's asskicking brand of hot. Bonus sexy: Watch to the end of this episode for that long-awaited lip-lock between Syd and Vaughn (Michael Vartan).

5 Y Tu Mamá También
2001

A drunken, boisterous celebration between two teens (Diego Luna and Gael García Bernal)

CONTINUES ON PAGE 120 ▶

MISSISSIPPI MASALA

and their older road-trip companion (Ana López Mercado) escalates into a sensuous three-way; as Mercado heads south of the border, the guys unexpectedly—and passionately—kiss.

6 The Last of the Mohicans
1992
Daniel Day-Lewis as a hunk?

Yes, indeed, as the long-haired, hard-bodied frontiersman Hawkeye who promises Madeleine Stowe's Cora "I will find you!" Moviegoers swooned when, at the fort, he seeks out Cora, gazes at her with blunt lust, then leads her to a nook where they engage in a make-out session both intense and tender.

7 NYPD Blue
season 4, 1996
After all the drama, the booze, and the attempted engagement, in "Unembraceable You," Diane (Kim Delaney) pays Bobby (Jimmy Smits) a visit and uses her most persuasive language to win him back. The good news is that it works: They tie the knot in season 5. The bad news? He dies in season 6.

8 A Walk on the Moon
1999
Is there a hippie hotter than Viggo Mortensen's Walker Jerome? With his tousled bed-head and give-peace-a-chance gentleness, the traveling blouse salesman gives Diane Lane's Pearl, a frustrated, married mother of two, her very own summer of love—most memorably, under a waterfall.

9 The Notebook
2004
This adaptation of the Nicholas Sparks novel is an electrically erotic weepfest, thanks to the longing exuded by Ryan Gosling and Rachel McAdams. Seven years after their first attempt to have sex is interrupted, the pair finally, repeatedly, get it on in the mansion Gosling has renovated as a tribute to the love he feared he'd lost forever.

10 Grey's Anatomy
season 2, 2006
The M.D.'s of Seattle Grace have graced us with many

CONTINUES ON PAGE 122 ▶

Most Romantic Gestures

- Steve Carell sells his toy collectibles to start a life with Catherine Keener, **THE 40-YEAR-OLD VIRGIN**

- Colin Firth buys Renée Zellweger a new diary, **BRIDGET JONES'S DIARY**

- Richard Gere climbs up the fire escape to reach Julia Roberts, **PRETTY WOMAN**

- Ellen Pompeo maps out a floor plan for Patrick Dempsey's dream house with candles, **GREY'S ANATOMY**

- Liv Tyler gives up immortality to stay with Viggo Mortensen, **THE LORD OF THE RINGS: THE RETURN OF THE KING**

- Adam Sandler boards Drew Barrymore's flight to croon "I Want to Grow Old With You" to her, **THE WEDDING SINGER**

- Cory Monteith puts Lea Michele on the train to New York so she can further her career, **GLEE**

- A spectral Patrick Swayze lifts a coin for Demi Moore, **GHOST**

- Heath Ledger finds and keeps

the shirts Jake Gyllenhaal saved from their first trip, **BROKEBACK MOUNTAIN**

- Robert Downey Jr. blows up his Iron Man suits for Gwyneth Paltrow, **IRON MAN 3**

- Larenz Tate offers up an impromptu beat poem to Nia Long, **LOVE JONES**

- Ellen Page fills Michael Cera's mailbox with his favorite orange Tic Tacs, **JUNO**

- Chris Messina dances for Mindy Kaling to Aaliyah's "Try Again," **THE MINDY PROJECT**

- The Beast gives book-loving Belle his library, **BEAUTY AND THE BEAST**

- Ralph Fiennes carries Kristin Scott Thomas out of the cave, **THE ENGLISH PATIENT**

- Audrey Tautou sets up a wild goose chase through Paris for Mathieu Kassovitz, **AMÉLIE**

- Glen Hansard buys Markéta Irglová a piano, **ONCE**

- Campbell Scott gives Kyra

Sedgwick a highly coveted garage-door opener, **SINGLES**

- Shane West helps Mandy Moore fulfill the items on her bucket list, **A WALK TO REMEMBER**

- Scott Patterson builds Lauren Graham a mini skating rink to restore her delight in winter, **GILMORE GIRLS**

- Gerard Butler leaves Hilary Swank 10 messages to be opened after his death, **P.S. I LOVE YOU**

- Colin Firth learns Portuguese so he can propose to Lúcia Moniz, **LOVE ACTUALLY**

- Kyle Chandler tells Connie Britton it's her turn to take her dream job in Philadelphia, **FRIDAY NIGHT LIGHTS**

- Heath Ledger sings "Can't Take My Eyes Off of You" to Julia Stiles and dances across the bleachers, **10 THINGS I HATE ABOUT YOU**

- Will Ferrell brings baker Maggie Gyllenhaal flours, **STRANGER THAN FICTION**

FRIENDS

13 ER
season 5, 1998

"Stuck on You" finds the original McDreamy, George Clooney, hopping into a bath with a bubble-covered Julianna Margulies. Who says doctors don't make house calls anymore?

14 Love & Basketball
2000

This hardwood romance about two longtime neighbors with b-ball talent understands that on the right woman, a sports bra is as alluring as anything sold at Victoria's Secret. When they're in college, tomboy Monica (Sanaa Lathan) and BMOC Quincy (Omar Epps) channel their competitive juices into a strip game of one-on-one enhanced by trash talk and hands-on defense.

15 My So-Called Life
pilot episode, 1994

Claire Danes' Angela gazes dreamily at Jared Leto's Jordan, a sensitive bad boy who doesn't

memorable moments in bed (Mer and George's weepy, oopsy-awkward one-night stand?). "Losing My Religion," however, titillated like no other: McDreamy (Patrick Dempsey) + Meredith (Ellen Pompeo) - black panties = best prom night ever.

11 Mississippi Masala
1991

Director Mira Nair tackles racism and romance in this Mississippi-set bayou drama. African-American Demetrius Williams (Denzel Washington) and Uganda-born Indian Meena (Sarita Choudhury) spark from the get-go, much to their families' dismay. When they hit the sheets at a beachside hotel hideaway, the camera lingers on their entwined extremities.

12 Unfaithful
2002

How hot is this drama about a bored suburbanite (Diane Lane) having an adulterous affair with a bookselling lothario (Olivier Martinez)? The wronged husband is played by Richard Gere. As the housewife heads for home on the train, she goes between guilt and giddiness while visualizing her first hedonistic liaison.

#1

chart position the Righteous Brothers' 1965 "Unchained Melody,"
featured in Ghost's *pottery scene, reached in 1990 in the U.K.*

even know the intelligent, radiant, but shy Angela exists. The yearning in her look and the ache in Danes' voice tell you everything about youthful desire.

16 Bound
1996

It could've been just a very stylish male fantasy. But the Wachowskis recruited bisexual erotic writer Susie Bright as a "sex consultant" to help give a realistic edge to the romantic relationship between Jennifer Tilly's Mafia moll and Gina Gershon's ex-con handywoman. Sexiest

moment? When Tilly shows Gershon that she, too, is useful with her hands.

17 Friends
season 2, 1995

Central Perk was steamy—and not just because of the coffee. In fact, this sitcom's seminal moment took place within the doors of the famed java joint, when Rachel (Jennifer Aniston) and Ross (David Schwimmer) shared a fervent, rain-soaked kiss in "The One Where Ross Finds Out."

CONTINUES ON PAGE 124 ▶

GHOST

Bonus!

Real-Life Couples With Great Screen Chemistry

Goldie Hawn and Kurt Russell, **SWING SHIFT** and **OVERBOARD**

Anna Paquin and Stephen Moyer, **TRUE BLOOD**

Brad Pitt and Angelina Jolie, **MR. AND MRS. SMITH**

Ginnifer Goodwin and Josh Dallas, **ONCE UPON A TIME**

Penélope Cruz and Javier Bardem, **VICKY CRISTINA BARCELONA**

Keri Russell and Matthew Rhys, **THE AMERICANS**

Emily VanCamp and Josh Bowman, **REVENGE**

Eva Mendes and Ryan Gosling, **THE PLACE BEYOND THE PINES**

Jennifer Aniston and Justin Theroux, **WANDERLUST**

Johnny Depp and Amber Heard, **THE RUM DIARY**

Sexiest Scenes With No Sex

Daniel Day-Lewis unbuttons Michelle Pfeiffer's glove, **THE AGE OF INNOCENCE**

Dakota Johnson and Jamie Dornan negotiate their contract, **FIFTY SHADES OF GREY**

Julie Delpy sings a song she's written for Ethan Hawke and tells him he's going to miss his plane, **BEFORE SUNSET**

Glen Hansard and Markéta Irglová collaborate on "Falling Slowly" in the music store, **ONCE**

Leonardo DiCaprio sketches Kate Winslet, **TITANIC**

LOST

21 The Bodyguard
1992

What's one of the hottest things an onscreen couple can do? Fight. Whitney Houston, playing a pop diva/movie star, and Kevin Costner, as her sullen bodyguard, do more than smolder and flirt—they square off like angry tigers. And when he carries her out of a club-gig-turned-riot, you know just why she throws her arms around her caveman protector.

22 The Bridges of Madison County
1995

There's nothing sexy about Robert James Waller's 1992 novella—192 pages of literary saltpeter. So it's a miracle that the onscreen chemistry between Clint Eastwood's globe-trotting photographer and Meryl Streep's shy farm wife winds up being so passionate, profound, and heartbreaking. Their romance's hottest moment is one of its quietest: late afternoon, two total

CONTINUES ON PAGE 126 ▶

18 Ghost
1990

What if, after your lover died, his soul stuck around to watch over you? The triumph of *Ghost*—starring Patrick Swayze as the specter and Demi Moore as the bereaved—is turning that kinda creepy premise into something sad yet sensual. The pottery wheel scene, played to the tune of "Unchained Melody," set a new standard for cinematic sensuality. (Fun fact: Moore's character was originally a woodworker.)

19 Thelma & Louise
1991

Rarely has a bare chest made such an impression or launched a more stellar career: Wolfish J.D. (Brad Pitt) and his washboard abs show sheltered Thelma (Geena Davis) "what all the fuss is about" with a motel fling that steals more than her innocence.

20 Lost
season 3, 2006

Being stranded on an island leaves lots of time for . . . getting to know one another intimately. In "I Do," Kate (Evangeline Lilly) and Sawyer (Josh Holloway) let loose during a pent-up, animalistic encounter in a polar bear cage.

POP CULTURE OBSESSION:

Stories About Show Biz

ANXIOUS ACTORS, SCUZZY AGENTS, MUSIC STARS
WHO RISE AND FALL—ENTERTAINERS HAVE ALWAYS
MADE FOR CLASSIC PLOTLINES

THE MUSIC WORLD

WHAT'S LOVE GOT TO DO WITH IT?
1993

KILL YOUR FRIENDS, BY JOHN NIVEN
2008

THE BODYGUARD
1992

DREAMGIRLS
2006

THE FIVE HEARTBEATS
1991

EMPIRE
2015

THE DOORS
1991

CRAZY HEART
2009

MY WEEK WITH MARILYN
2011

ED WOOD
1994

CHAPLIN
1992

ACTORS AND DIRECTORS

GODS AND MONSTERS
1998

BIRDMAN
2014

MAN ON THE MOON
1999

THE ARTIST

HITCHCOCK
2012

THE PLAYER
1992

SWIMMING WITH SHARKS
1994

SAVING MR. BANKS
2013

THE BUSINESS OF HOLLYWOOD

FORCE MAJEURE, BY
BRUCE WAGNER
1991

GET SHORTY
1995

THE COMEDY WRITER, BY
PETER FARRELLY
1998

STUDIO 60 ON THE SUNSET STRIP
2006-7

THE TV SET
2006

MORNING GLORY
2010

TELEVISION

strangers making dinner together. Seriously.

23 The Tudors
season 1, 2007

Jonathan Rhys Meyers' King Henry VIII just can't get enough. Anne Boleyn (Natalie Dormer) wants a ring. So episode 10's clandestine meeting in the woods is frustration and passion personified.

24 The Talented Mr. Ripley
1999

A character is defined by what he wants . . . and what he'll do to get it. For Tom Ripley (Matt Damon), his greatest desire is to be as close as possible to Dickie Greenleaf (Jude Law), a layabout who makes everything—even tanning—an act of idle seduction. When Tom

and Dickie play a simple game of chess—over a bathtub, with Law naked inside—every move is an advance and a rebuff. Nothing that steamy ever ends well.

25 How Stella Got Her Groove Back
1998

As Winston Shakespeare,

Taye Diggs seduces the 20-year-older Stella (an ageless Angela Bassett) with his smooth Jamaican accent and equally smooth bod. Their steamy postfight shower romp is just one of many perfectly choreographed sex scenes that made women everywhere want to jet to Jamaica to get their own grooves back. ∎

The 25 Unsexiest Sex Scenes We Can't Unsee

SHOWGIRLS 1995 Elizabeth Berkley and Kyle MacLachlan have a pool party | **BODY OF EVIDENCE** 1993 Madonna waxes Willem Dafoe | **EYES WIDE SHUT** 1999 Tom Cruise goes to an orgy | **GET HIM TO THE GREEK** 2010 Jonah Hill gets acquainted with a dildo | **HOLY SMOKE** 1999 Harvey Keitel and Kate Winslet have deprogramming sex | All encounters in the **FIFTY SHADES OF GREY** "playroom" 2015 | **GONE GIRL** 2014 Rosamund Pike gets medieval on Neil Patrick Harris' ass | **ABOUT SCHMIDT** 2002 Kathy Bates and Jack Nicholson go hot-tubbing | **KNOCKED UP** 2007 Seth Rogen and Katherine Heigl make a big mistake | **GIGLI** 2003 Ben Affleck and Jennifer Lopez go "gobble, gobble" | **ALEXANDER** 2004 Colin Farrell and Rosario Dawson's overly energetic passion | **BOOGIE NIGHTS** 1997 Backseat sex with Roller Girl | **TEETH** 2007 Jess Weixler embodies a man's worst nightmare | **GIRLS** 2012 Lena Dunham and Adam Driver's all-too-real bad sex scenes | **MASTERS OF SEX** 2013 Any lovemaking involving electrodes | **THE DREAMERS** 2003 It's a threesome Michael Pitt, Eva Green, and Louis Garrel—with twins! | **THE PAPERBOY** 2012 Nicole Kidman gives John Cusack a thrill in prison | **CRASH** 1996 Rosanna Arquette seduces James Spader by showing off her scars | **SWORDFISH** 2001 The blow-job-at-gunpoint | **A HISTORY OF VIOLENCE** 2005 Viggo Mortensen and Maria Bello do it on the stairs | **THE COUNSELOR** 2013 Cameron Diaz mounts the windshield of a car | **SHOOT 'EM UP** 2007 Clive Owen's not shooting blanks with Monica Bellucci | **IN THE CUT** 2003 Meg Ryan and Mark Ruffalo's creepy liaison | **CRANK** 2006 Jason Statham and Amy Smart give a matinee performance in the middle of a Chinatown street | **LOUIE** 2012 Louis C.K.'s blind date Melissa Leo insists on oral-sex reciprocity

Onscreen Weddings

TALK ABOUT ALTARED STATES! THESE COUPLES' BIG DAYS RANGED FROM COMEDIC TO DRAMATIC . . . OR AWFUL

MOST DISASTROUS

The Bride's wedding, *Kill Bill*

Ross and Emily, *Friends*

Carrie and Big's canceled ceremony, the *Sex and the City* movie

The Red Wedding, *Game of Thrones*

Jake and Betsy, *Betsy's Wedding*

Booth and Brennan, *Bones*

Greg and Pam, *Meet the Fockers*

Jeremy and Gloria, *Wedding Crashers*

Turk and Carla, *Scrubs*

Michael and Kimberly, *My Best Friend's Wedding*

Jack and Betsy, *Honeymoon in Vegas*

Mitch and Cam, *Modern Family*

Maggie and Ike, *Runaway Bride*

Leslie and Ben, *Parks and Recreation*

LEAST DISASTROUS

Frank and Marissa, *Old School*

Muriel and David, *Muriel's Wedding*

Aditi and Hemant, *Monsoon Wedding*

Edward and Bella, *The Twilight Saga: Breaking Dawn—Part 1*

Kevin and Scotty, *Brothers and Sisters*

Sarah and Hank, *Parenthood*

Claire and Jamie, *Outlander*

Jim and Pam, *The Office*

Callie and Arizona, *Grey's Anatomy*

Lily and Marshall, *How I Met Your Mother*

Toula and Ian, *My Big Fat Greek Wedding*

LEAST HEARTWARMING

MOST HEARTWARMING

Late Night COMEDY MOMENTS

WITH HILARIOUS SKITS, REOCCURRING BITS, MUSIC VIDEOS, AND JAW–DROPPING INTERVIEWS,
THESE HOSTS STARTED WITH A MONOLOGUE AND THEN WENT ABOVE AND BEYOND

1. FALLON
GETS DOWN
WITH MICHELLE
OBAMA

In an epic lip-synch show-down, the head-bobbing, rapid-rapping *Amazing Spider-Man* actress got an assist from an overhead camera as her hands went UP for DJ Khaled's "All I Do Is Win." Jimmy, with his silly "Mr. Roboto," didn't stand a chance.

3 Jimmy Goes to Bayside

The Tonight Show Starring Jimmy Fallon, Feb. 4, 2015
After years of lobbying, Fallon reunited the cast of the '90s zit-com *Saved by the Bell* (with bonus Mr. Belding). In a sketch set at Bayside High, Jimmy donned a shaggy wig, Mark-Paul Gosselaar called a "time-out," Tiffani Thiessen donned a cheerleader outfit, and Mario Lopez busted out his dance moves.

JIMMY FALLON MOMENTS

1 Fallon Gets Down With Michelle Obama

Late Night With Jimmy Fallon,
Feb. 22, 2013

To promote her Let's Move campaign, the First Lady got into a funky pas-de-dude with Jimmy, who donned a wig and pink cardigan to demonstrate the evolution of "mom dancing"—from the "Driving the Station Wagon" to "The 'Pulp Fiction.'"

2 Emma Stone Goes Up on Jimmy

The Tonight Show Starring Jimmy Fallon, April 28, 2014

---

4 Nothing Like a Damon

Jimmy Kimmel Live!
Jan. 31, 2008
Sarah Silverman was still dating Kimmel when she stopped by with a music-video confession: that she was, ahem, f---ing his long-time Hollywood punching boy, Matt Damon. In song: "On a bed, on the floor, on a towel by the door."

5 Mr. Hot Stuff

Jimmy Kimmel Live!
March 7, 2010
On his post-Oscar show, Kimmel assembled a 12-pack of Hollywood's hottest guys—including Rob Lowe, Matthew McConaughey, and Lenny Kravitz—to preside over a meeting of the Handsome Men's Club. Matt Damon, naturally, had the last laugh.

6 How Tweet It Isn't

Jimmy Kimmel Live!
March 2012–present
Twitter was six years old when Kimmel launched one of his most popular recurring bits, with stars from Julia Roberts to Barack Obama reciting some of the snarkier Tweets about their career or, in the president's case, choice of jeans.

CONTINUES ON PAGE 131 ▶

4. NOTHING LIKE A DAMON

Bonus!

Traumatic Thanksgivings

FRIENDS, "The One With All the Thanksgivings"	SEASON 5
BUFFY THE VAMPIRE SLAYER, "Pangs"	SEASON 4
GILMORE GIRLS, "A Deep-Fried Korean Thanksgiving"	SEASON 3
HOW I MET YOUR MOTHER, "Slapsgiving"	SEASON 3
HOME FOR THE HOLIDAYS	1995

Climactic Christmases

SEINFELD, "The Strike" (the Festivus episode)	SEASON 9
THE O.C., "The Best Chrismukkah Ever"	SEASON 1
30 ROCK, "Ludachristmas"	SEASON 2
THE OFFICE (UK), THE CHRISTMAS SPECIAL	2003
ARRESTED DEVELOPMENT, "Afternoon Delight"	SEASON 2
COMMUNITY, "Abed's Uncontollable Christmas"	SEASON 2
THE OFFICE, "Christmas Party"	SEASON 2
ALLY MCBEAL, "Blue Christmas"	SEASON 3
THE FAMILY STONE	2005
ELF	2003
THE MUPPET CHRISTMAS CAROL	1992
THE WEST WING, "In Excelsis Deo"	SEASON 1

Neurotic New Year's

HOW I MET YOUR MOTHER, "The Limo"	SEASON 1
THE O.C., "The Countdown"	SEASON 1

Fraught Fourths of July

INDEPENDENCE DAY	1996
LIVE FREE OR DIE HARD	2007

Big Birthdays

PARTY DOWN, "Steve Guttenberg's Birthday"	SEASON
13 GOING ON 30	2004
FRIENDS, "The One Where They All Turn Thirty"	SEASON 7
THE OFFICE, "Michael's Birthday"	SEASON 2

Stephen Colbert

MASTER SATIRIST, COINER OF WORDS, SINGER, DANCER, PRESIDENTIAL CANDIDATE—AND NOW *LATE SHOW* HOST. IF TRUTHINESS BE TOLD, HIS IMPACT HAS BEEN WIDE AND WEIGHTY.

9
years he hosted *The Colbert Report*

6
Emmys won by *The Colbert Report*

9
Emmys he's won himself (including 3 for *The Daily Show*)

1,447
episodes of *The Colbert Report*

2
Grammys he's won: Best Comedy Album, for *A Colbert Christmas* (2010); Best Spoken World Album for *America Again: Re-Becoming the Greatness We Never Weren't* (2014)

3
presidents who were guests on *The Colbert Report* (Obama, Clinton, and Carter)

3/20/07
date Stephen Colbert Day was celebrated in Oshawa, Ontario

9/8/15
air date of the first *Late Show with Stephen Colbert*

105
guest stars on the final episode of *The Colbert Report* (not including staff)

2006
year he was headliner at the White House Correspondents' Dinner

2010
year the Colbert-coined "TRUTHINESS" was added to the *New Oxford American Dictionary*

77 %
percentage of people who responded yes to a 2012 poll asking if his calling Windsor, Ontario, "the Earth's rectum" was good for the city

ZERO
times he's hosted *SNL* (though he was the voice of Ace, in the show's Ambiguously Gay Duo cartoon, for years)

$300,000+

RAISED FOR THE U.S. OLYMPIC SPEED-SKATING TEAM BY THE COLBERT NATION

13.4%

percentage of times he once joked that he agreed with his Colbert character

10

siblings he grew up with (he was the youngest of 11)

16

Days he was officially running for president in the fall of 2007

8.5 MILLION

Twitter followers

ONE

episode of *Law & Order: Criminal Intent* appeared on, in 2004

1

piece of equipment on the International Space Station named after him: the Combined Operational Load-Bearing External Resistance Treadmill

215,000

people estimated to have attended his and Jon Stewart's "Rally to Restore Sanity and/or Fear" in Washington, D.C., in 2010

EIGHT

years Ben & Jerry's AmeriCone Dream ice cream has been available; Colbert's proceeds from its sale support a variety of causes

1,120

calories in a pint of AmeriCone Dream

2

times he's been named one of *Time*'s 100 Most Influential People in the World (in 2006 and 2012)

24

weeks his 2007 book *I Am America (And So Can You!)* was on the *New York Times* hardcover nonfiction bestseller list (No. 1 for 14 of them)

CONTINUED FROM PAGE 129

STEPHEN COLBERT MOMENTS

7 The Whole Truthiness

The Colbert Report, Oct. 17, 2005

It didn't take long for Stephen Colbert to change the lexicon—and coin a *Merriam-Webster*-certified Word of the Year. In his pilot episode, he used truthiness to describe the squishy "gut feelings" that led to political decisions like the 2003 invasion of Iraq.

8 A Kick in the Hashtag

The Colbert Report, March 31, 2014

After a context-free joke about Asians was posted on the show's official Twitter feed, "the Twit hit the fan." #CancelColbert became a trending topic. Colbert's mea culpa offered a view from inside the eye of a media-fed tornado of faux controversy.

9 Colbert Suqs Up

The Colbert Report, Aug. 4, 2011

Starting his own Super-PAC was simultaneously informative and hilarious. But when he announced that the PAC's contributors included an Arab American named Suq Madiq, Colbert's famous stoicism cracked behind a burst of school-boy giggles.

10 Daft Punk'd

The Colbert Report, Aug. 6, 2013

Who cares if the French electronica duo Daft Punk really canceled an appearance? It's viewers who got lucky as Colbert filled time with an ever-more-elaborate dance-party video featuring Jeff Bridges, the Rockettes, Matt Damon, and even Henry Kissinger.

CONTINUES ON PAGE 132 ▶

drinks Steve Carell consumed in the first hour of his
marathon boozing session on The Daily Show

7

JON STEWART

....

JON STEWART MOMENTS

....

11 **Life of O'Reilly**
The Daily Show,
Sept. 27, 2010
Stewart greeted Bill O'Reilly on his home turf for a jocular and pointed exchange. Even better: the post-interview analysis by Olivia Munn and John Oliver, who described Stewart as "cowering and insect-like" before the physically bigger Fox News host.

12 **Drink Responsibly**
The Daily Show,

March 27, 2001
To demonstrate the effects of binge drinking, correspondent Steve Carell headed to a bar with a sober Stephen Colbert and got increasingly blotto. He knocked over glasses, shoved Colbert, shed his shirt, and later confessed to vomiting on the car ride home.

....

DAVID LETTERMAN MOMENTS

....

13 **Drew's Birthday Suit**
The Late Show With David Letterman, April 12, 1995
It was the ultimate birthday

12. DRINK RESPONSIBLY

11:12

13. DREW'S BIRTHDAY SUIT

present. After chatting about the "nude art-performance dance place" she frequented, a 20-year-old Drew Barrymore shimmied atop Letterman's desk and lifted her "I'm bananas" T-shirt to flash him her breasts.

14 Joaquin Checks Out

The Late Show With David Letterman, Feb. 11, 2009
A disturbingly out-of-it Joaquin Phoenix, sporting dark glasses and a ZZ Top-like beard, chewed gum and mum-

bled his way through nine minutes of awkwardness. It turned out to be a hoax, a stunt for his mockumentary *I'm Still Here*, but it's still riveting TV.

15 Dave Raises McCain

The Late Show With David Letterman, Sept. 24, 2008
It was bad enough for John McCain on the eve of the 2008 election to cancel an appearance at the last minute. But when Letterman learned

CONTINUES ON PAGE 134 ▶

$ITCOM LIFE$TYLE$

SOME FLASHED THEIR CASH, WHILE OTHERS PINCHED PENNIES

ENTOURAGE

VEEP

THE NANNY

TWO AND A HALF MEN

FRASIER

30 ROCK

SPIN CITY

MODERN FAMILY

WILL & GRACE

BLACK-ISH

THE FRESH PRINCE OF BEL-AIR

MAD ABOUT YOU

SEINFELD

FRIENDS

SEX AND THE CITY

EVERYBODY LOVES RAYMOND

HOME IMPROVEMENT

THE OFFICE

MIKE AND MOLLY

THE KING OF QUEENS

IT'S ALWAYS SUNNY IN PHILADELPHIA

MARRIED…WITH CHILDREN

ROSEANNE

THE MIDDLE

2 BROKE GIRLS

RICH

NO MONEY TROUBLES

SCRAPING BY

The Wayfarers Bill Clinton wore during his groundbreaking sax performance were senior campaign strategist Paul Begala's. They were donated to the Clinton Library.

17. BILL CLINTON'S SAX LIFE

"Heartbreak Hotel," cementing his rep as a next-generation pol. As Hall presciently quipped, "It's nice to see a Democrat blow something besides the election."

18 Interviewing an Ax Murderer

The Arsenio Hall Show, July 28, 1989
"The term 'deranged sociopath' gets thrown around a lot by the media," Hall said, "but it really applies to my next guest." Thus began an uproarious one-sided interview with the ax-wielding, hockey-masked Jason Voorhees (Kane Hodder) from the *Friday the 13th* horror series.

mid-taping that the Republican was nearby taping an interview with Katie Couric, his dudgeon rose to new comic heights.

16 Combative Material Girl

The Late Show With David Letterman, March 31, 1994

Long a monologue punchline, a spirited Madonna turned up for a notoriously prickly interview bearing a gift—a pair of her underwear. She proceeded to drop the F-bomb as well as a string of insults to Letterman, who seemed both fired up and fearful.

ARSENIO HALL MOMENTS

17 Bill Clinton's Sax Life

The Arsenio Hall Show, June 2, 1992
Candidate Bill Clinton took his saxophone and shades to late night and tooted out

CONAN O'BRIEN MOMENTS

19 Conando Es Caliente

The Tonight Show With Conan O'Brien, June 8, 2009
During his short-lived *Tonight Show* tenure, L.A. transplant Conan O'Brien decided to stage a telenovela to lure

Latino viewers—and the first segment included a troublesome live horse, a wandering mustache, and a mariachi-clad Andy Richter. *"Caballo estúpido, Conando."*

20 The Domino's Effect

The Tonight Show With Conan O'Brien, Aug. 13, 2009

In a nod to a famed segment from Johnny Carson's era at *The Tonight Show*, O'Brien enlisted a small army of uniformed Domino's Pizza employees to create a human falling domino trick.

21 Sarah Palin, Beat Poet

The Tonight Show With Conan O'Brien, Dec. 11, 2009

Months after William Shatner recited passages from Sarah Palin's speeches as beat poetry (complete with bongo-drum accompaniment), the Alaska Republican gamely came on to deliver her own recitation from the actor's memoir.

SNL MOMENTS

22 Laser LOL Cats

Saturday Night Live, April 15, 2006

Bill Hader and Andy Samberg tried to persuade Lorne Michaels to air their micro-micro-budget sci-fi short featuring cats (both live and stuffed) who shoot lasers out of their mouths. Five years later, Tom Hanks and Elton John joined in an equally silly musical version.

23 Once a Year. Period.

Saturday Night Live, Feb. 23, 2008

In a fake ad for hormone pills that let a woman have her period just once a year, all's sweetness until the warning about the supersize effects of that saved-up event: Tina Fey wielded an ax on

CONTINUES ON PAGE 136 ▶

22. LASER LOL CATS

LATE NIGHT COMEDY MOMENTS CONTINUED FROM PAGE 135

25. SUPREME COURT GOES TO THE DOGS

colleagues while Kristen Wiig French-kissed a dog.

24 Who Needs Baby Fat?

Saturday Night Live,
Oct. 23, 2010

"Do you have a fat baby? Are you ashamed of it?" asked Jason Sudeikis as a spokesman for Baby Spanx, a godsend for parents Bill Hader and Kristen Wiig anxious to have a more fab, slimmed-down newborn. "I would never spank a baby. But I sure as hell would Spanx one."

....
JOHN OLIVER MOMENTS
....

25 Supreme Court Goes to the Dogs

Last Week Tonight With John Oliver, Oct. 19, 2014

Peeved that the Supreme Court won't allow videotaping of its oral arguments, John Oliver re-created the nation's highest court using real dogs and fake paws, gesturing dramatically to real audio recordings. Bonus: a chicken pecked at a transcription machine. ∎

THE BULLSEYE

Screen Deaths

HERE'S A LOOK AT THE HIGH-PROFILE DEMISES THAT WERE RIGHT ON TARGET—AND SOME THAT MISSED THE MARK

1	THE GOOD WIFE	Will gets caught in the crossfire
2	JURASSIC PARK	First, kill the lawyer
3	SEINFELD	Takes a (stamp) licking, doesn't keep on ticking
4	BRAVEHEART	"Freeeeedom!"
5	FARGO	Feeding the woodchipper
6	SONS OF ANARCHY	Gemma's execution
7	SHERLOCK	Holmes takes a leap of faith
8	THIRTYSOMETHING	Gary never makes it to the hospital
9	LA LAW	Rosalind Shays get shafted
10	HOMELAND	Brody's public hanging
11	DEAD LIKE ME	George has trouble with a toilet
12	HOUSE OF CARDS	Zoe takes the subway
13	GOODFELLAS	Tommy loses his hair-trigger temper
14	CLIFFHANGER	A rescue goes wrong
15	KILL BILL VOL. 1	O-Ren discovers "that really was a Hattori Hanzo sword"
16	THE SOPRANOS	Big Pussy sleeps with the fishes
17	ER	Dr. Greene goes over the rainbow in Hawaii
18	NYPD BLUE	Bobby's heart gives way
19	GAME OF THRONES	Ned Stark loses his head
20	THE WIRE	Omar buys it in a convenience store
21	MAD MEN	Lane hangs himself in the office
22	GOLDENEYE	Xenia Onatopp has legs and knows how to use them
23	INDEPENDENCE DAY	A heroic kamikaze pilot targets the alien ship
24	TOTAL RECALL	"Consider that a divorce"
25	THELMA & LOUISE	Hurtling into the Grand Canyon

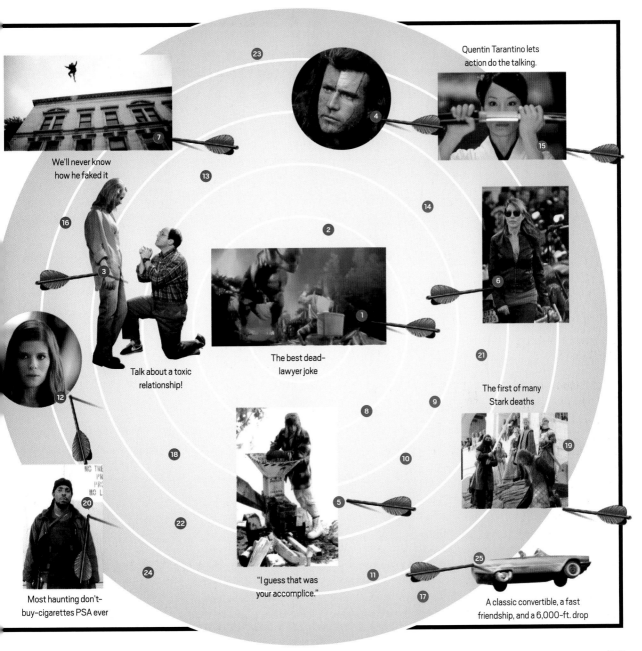

Quentin Tarantino lets action do the talking.

We'll never know how he faked it

The best dead-lawyer joke

Talk about a toxic relationship!

The first of many Stark deaths

"I guess that was your accomplice."

Most haunting don't-buy-cigarettes PSA ever

A classic convertible, a fast friendship, and a 6,000-ft. drop

Special Effects

THE LAST 25 YEARS HAVE SEEN A REVOLUTION IN VISUAL FX—AND MADE THESE THRILLING MOVIE MOMENTS POSSIBLE

TERMINATOR 2

1 Terminator 2: Judgment Day

1991

Digital effects had only barely been invented when James Cameron decided to meld practical effects and the new tech, and made his sequel bad guy a CGI shape-changer. The body-morphing result sparked a generation of liquid-gooey imitators.

2 Jurassic Park

1993

Often regarded as the official beginning of the computer-effects era, Steven Spielberg's dino romp is actually the perfect Venn Diagram merging of practical effects and CGI. Just look at the T. Rex. Sometimes it's a model; sometimes it's CGI. Those raptors in the kitchen? An actor wearing one of Stan Winston Studio's elaborate costumes. The end result is just plain terrifying.

3 The Matrix
1999

Devotees of Hong Kong action cinema and video-game aesthetics, the Wachowskis merged their influences into Bullet Time,

JURASSIC PARK

the slow-motion tracking shot created using elaborate multi-camera rigs.

4 Tremors
1990

The last great creature feature of the predigital era, *Tremors'* underground graboid monsters are grotesquely phallic gigantic worms. Only one life-size model was created— and in the grand tradition of *Jaws*, the monsters are most scary when they're off screen.

5 Hollow Man
2000

Playing invisible used to be so simple. Then came the green-screen era. Kevin Bacon spent most of production in a head-to-toe body suit. It's a thankless performance—he's literally not even on screen most of the time— but a visual marvel.

6 Life of Pi
2012

Few CGI effects are harder

CONTINUES ON PAGE 141 ▶

25 Fun Flashback Films

REVISIT THESE ERAS—NO TIME MACHINE NEEDED

1960s
ACROSS THE UNIVERSE
CATCH ME IF YOU CAN
DREAMGIRLS
INSIDE LLEWYN DAVIS
AUSTIN POWERS: THE SPY WHO SHAGGED ME
BACKBEAT
THE DOORS
SELMA
I SHOT ANDY WARHOL

1970s
DAZED AND CONFUSED
AMERICAN HUSTLE
DONNIE BRASCO
ALMOST FAMOUS
ANCHORMAN
SUMMER OF SAM

1980s
24 HOUR PARTY PEOPLE
AMERICAN PSYCHO
BOOGIE NIGHTS
ADVENTURELAND
LAST DAYS OF DISCO
THE WEDDING SINGER
WET HOT AMERICAN SUMMER

1990s
RENT
NOTORIOUS
THE WOLF OF WALL STREET

James Cameron

THIS VISIONARY PERFECTIONIST HAS UPPED THE ANTE ON SPECIAL EFFECTS WITH HIS HUGELY INFLUENTIAL SCI-FI AND DISASTER FILMS

six

OSCAR NOMINATIONS

(for *Titanic* and *Avatar*)

3

OSCAR WINS

(for *Titanic*)

14

age when he saw *2001: A Space Odyssey* and knew that he wanted to make his own films

1982

year he had a dream about a chrome skeleton emerging out of a fire; it became 1984's *The Terminator*

1

Razzie he's won (Worst Screenplay for 1985's *Rambo: First Blood Part II*)

one

TV series he's created, *Dark Angel*

5

FILMS HE'S DONE WITH BILL PAXTON: *The Terminator, Aliens, True Lies, Titanic, Ghosts of the Abyss*

4

directors who've cited Cameron's work as an inspiration: Joss Whedon, Peter Jackson, Baz Luhrmann, and Michael Bay

3

sequels to *Avatar* he plans to film simultaneously, to be released December 2017, 2018, and 2019

500

approximate number of words created for the Na'vi language in *Avatar*, by linguist Paul Frommer

$2.7 MILLION

price he paid for the Beaufort Vineyard and Estate Winery in British Columbia

2012

year he became a vegan (along with his wife and children)

70%

percentage of *Avatar* that's CGI

24
identical versions made of the dress Kate Winslet wears the night the *Titanic* sinks

80
Titanic cast and crew members (including Cameron) who unknowingly ate PCP-piked lobster chowder one night (no suspects were found)

1000+
total number of extras in *Titanic*

$7 BILLION

WORLDWIDE GROSS
OF HIS FILMS

36
hours
length of the first cut of *Titanic*

3 hours 23 minutes
Titanic's final running time

2004
year Cameron, a Canadian citizen, withdrew his application for American citizenship (because George W. Bush won the election)

1
species of frog named after him, Venezuela's *Pristimantis jamescameroni*

3
feet
depth of the water many of *Titanic*'s ocean scenes were filmed in

3
times he went down to the wreck of *Titanic* (at 12,500 feet)

55
feet
depth of the underwater filming in *The Abyss*

6.8
miles (35,904 feet) he descended in the Mariana Trench, the deepest known area of the world's oceans. He was the first to do a solo descent, in a submersible vessel he designed

10K
20K
30K
40K

CONTINUED FROM PAGE 139

than hair: all those infinitesimal shafts, the light dappling off every one. Which makes it more impressive that Ang Lee set out to make his seaward epic with a digital tiger—a furry costar created entirely from pixels.

7 Interstellar
2014
When you're creating a wormhole, it helps to have a theoretical physicist on your team. Scientist Kip Thorne helped the effects team explore *Interstellar*'s cosmic ideas.

8 Forrest Gump
1994
This film's best effect is literally invisible: Costar Gary Sinise wore blue-screen fabric around his legs to play double-amputee Lieutenant Dan.

9 Titanic
1997
Cameron started off as a

special effects technician. For his sinking-ship masterpiece, he used every trick in the book. The climactic moment when *Titanic* cracks in two required a massive tilting set, a hundred stunt-people, and CGI.

10 The Curious Case of Benjamin Button
2008
Only David Fincher would take Brad Pitt—generally considered one of the finer specimens of human beauty—and transform him into a wrinkly, decrepit old toddler.

11 Babe
1995
Real live animals did the "acting" in this farm-house fairy tale by George Miller and Chris Noonan. In postproduction, special effects engineers applied some innovative

CONTINUES ON PAGE 142 ▶

"If you think too much about what's doable, you'll have scissors in your head." — *Roland Emmerich, director/cowriter,* The Day After Tomorrow

THE LORD OF
THE RINGS

14 The Lord of the Rings

2001, 2002, 2003

Andy Serkis became the first superstar of the performance capture era playing Gollum, the poignantly insane ring addict. Gollum was the killer app for CGI: proof that computer effects could enhance humanity, not just replace it.

15 Death Becomes Her

1992

Director Robert Zemeckis is best known for elaborate adventures, but this raucous immortality farce features his Hall of Fame visual: Meryl Streep's head twisted backward on her body.

16 Independence Day

1996

The defining image of cinematic destruction was created using old-fashioned explosives and a model of the White House 10 feet wide. It's still stunning—and, today, horrifically resonant.

computer modeling over their jawline, creating human-like talking "mouths" over the original animals.

12 Pirates of the Caribbean: The Curse of the Black Pearl

2003

Disney's Pirates of the Caribbean ride was a legendary ritual for generations of kids—at once scary and delightful, it was a morbidly funny G-rated horror show. Director Gore Verbinski translated that sensibility perfectly with *Black Pearl*'s living skeletons: anatomically detailed, ghoulishly organic, yet animated with a playful touch.

13 The Day After Tomorrow

2004

Not satisfied with destroying the White House in *Independence Day*, Roland Emmerich took on the rest of the world in his global-warming epic. In the craziest moment, a tsunami wave hits Manhattan; you'll never look at the Hudson the same way again.

17 Pan's Labyrinth
2006

Contortionist and monster actor Doug Jones played two characters in Guillermo Del Toro's horrific bedtime story: the beckoning freaky-but-friendly Faun and the faceless all-devouring Pale Man. Their elegant prosthetic designs made them creepy, yet haunting beautiful—and Jones' performance gave both a soul.

18 Twister
1996

We can all agree that those digital tornadoes look cool. Heck, the plot of *Twister* is mostly just people admiring those tornadoes. But can we talk about that flying cow?

19 Harry Potter and the Deathly Hallows Part 2
2011

No stops were left unpulled out for *Harry Potter*'s wizard war, a fireworks display of spells and attack-magick featuring every far-flung member of the franchise's cast. From the explosive Fiendfyre scene in the Room of Requirement to Harry and Voldy's epic duel, few battles have felt more final.

CONTINUES ON PAGE 144 ▶

PAN'S LABYRINTH

Very Dysfunctional Families

THEY'RE CREEPY, KOOKY, AND SOMETIMES DECIDEDLY SPOOKY

FAMILY	SHOW
The Lannisters	GAME OF THRONES
The Gallaghers	SHAMELESS
The Dollangangers	FLOWERS IN THE ATTIC
The Lyonses	EMPIRE
The Bateses	BATES MOTEL
The Bluths	ARRESTED DEVELOPMENT
The Ewings	DALLAS
The Dillons	THE GRIFTERS
The Bundys	MARRIED...WITH CHILDREN
The Tellers and the Morrows	SONS OF ANARCHY
The Tenenbaums	THE ROYAL TENENBAUMS
The Fishers	SIX FEET UNDER
The Fangs	THE FAMILY FANG
The Beales	GREY GARDENS
The Burnhams	AMERICAN BEAUTY
The Reynoldses	IT'S ALWAYS SUNNY IN PHILADELPHIA
The Lamberts	THE CORRECTIONS
The Middlesteins	THE MIDDLESTEINS
The Drapers	MAD MEN
The Foxmans	THIS IS WHERE I LEAVE YOU
The Chasseurs	THE REF
The Chances	RAISING HOPE
The Hoods and the Carvers	THE ICE STORM
The Berkmans	THE SQUID AND THE WHALE
The Plunketts	MOM

DECADES OF THERAPY

COULD BE WORSE

CONTINUED FROM PAGE 143

20 Starship Troopers
1997

Legendary monster-meister Phil Tippett created the memorable creatures in *Return of the Jedi* and *Dragonslayer*. A decade later, he led the studio to create the extraterrestrial Arachnid hordes on Klendathu. The result: nightmare swarms of sinewy monstrosities, like *Saving Private Ryan*'s D-Day sequence for cockroaches.

21 Transformers
2007

The special effects pioneers at Industrial Light & Magic turned Michael Bay's robo-car franchise into a sizzle reel for intricate CGI. Their finest creation: the heroic Autobot commander Optimus Prime, a gigantic posthuman super-hero rendered with lovingly elaborate gearhead detail.

22 Inception
2010

Christopher Nolan is Hollywood's reigning digital

AVATAR

skeptic, preferring to shoot practical effects on old-fashioned film. So the hotel-corridor scene in *Inception* required devilishly complicated sets, rotating the actors on wires and steel trolleys. The result is an old-fashioned "how'd they do that?" delight.

23 Gravity
2013

There's not much gravity in *Gravity*, and Sandra Bullock spent whole days inside a high-tech rig to create the

illusion of weightlessness. Might've been easier just to go to space.

24 The Perfect Storm
2000

Digital effects can create worlds undreamed of, but in this true-life disaster blockbuster, Wolfgang Petersen takes a different path. The climactic CGI wave isn't fantasy; it's horrifying, vividly real, a vision of nature run amok.

25 Avatar
2009

Eighteen years after the T-1000, James Cameron's most recent biggest-budget-ever odyssey featured an entire world of digital characters. Captured in bold 3D, Cameron's Pandora is the epitome of the computer effects era. What you may not know: The vision of the Na'Vi was first captured in clay by sculptor and concept artist Jordu Schell. Hold tight: At least three more *Avatars* are coming soon. ■

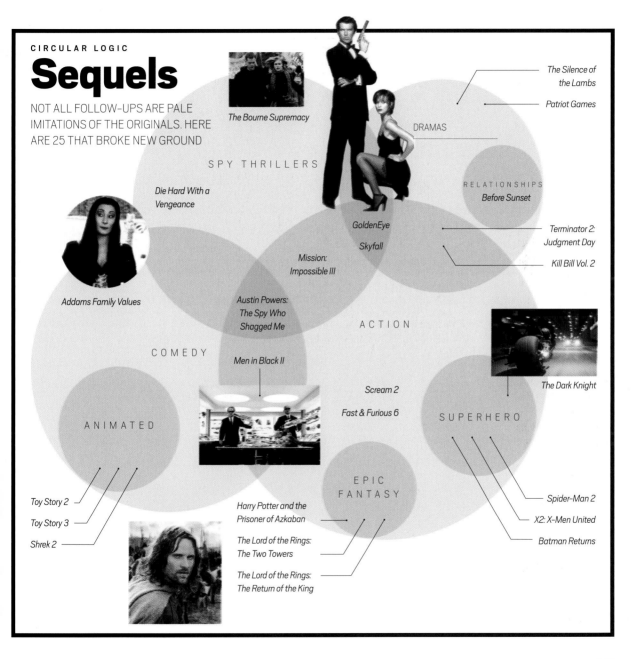

Sequels

NOT ALL FOLLOW-UPS ARE PALE
IMITATIONS OF THE ORIGINALS. HERE
ARE 25 THAT BROKE NEW GROUND

The Bourne Supremacy

DRAMAS

SPY THRILLERS

*The Silence of
the Lambs*

Patriot Games

RELATIONSHIPS
Before Sunset

*Die Hard With a
Vengeance*

GoldenEye

Skyfall

*Terminator 2:
Judgment Day*

*Mission:
Impossible III*

Kill Bill Vol. 2

Addams Family Values

*Austin Powers:
The Spy Who
Shagged Me*

ACTION

COMEDY

Men in Black II

The Dark Knight

Scream 2

Fast & Furious 6

SUPERHERO

ANIMATED

EPIC
FANTASY

Toy Story 2

Toy Story 3

Shrek 2

*Harry Potter and the
Prisoner of Azkaban*

*The Lord of the Rings:
The Two Towers*

*The Lord of the Rings:
The Return of the King*

Spider-Man 2

X2: X-Men United

Batman Returns

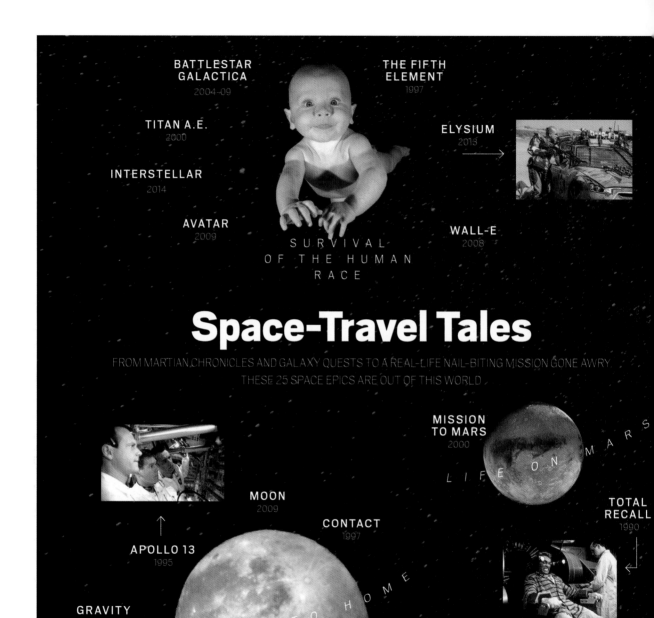

BATTLESTAR GALACTICA
2004–09

THE FIFTH ELEMENT
1997

TITAN A.E.
2000

ELYSIUM
2013

INTERSTELLAR
2014

AVATAR
2009

SURVIVAL OF THE HUMAN RACE

WALL-E
2008

Space-Travel Tales

FROM MARTIAN CHRONICLES AND GALAXY QUESTS TO A REAL-LIFE NAIL-BITING MISSION GONE AWRY,
THESE 25 SPACE EPICS ARE OUT OF THIS WORLD

MISSION TO MARS
2000

LIFE ON MARS

MOON
2009

TOTAL RECALL
1990

APOLLO 13
1995

CONTACT
1997

GRAVITY
2013

CLOSER TO HOME

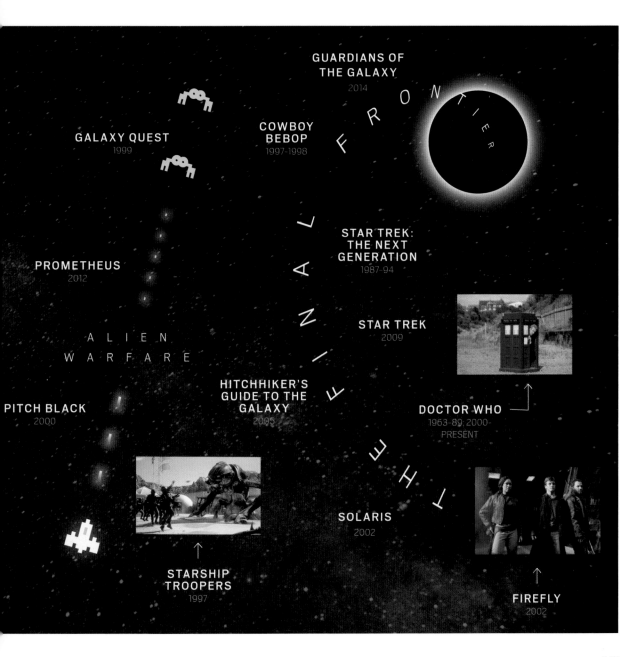

GUARDIANS OF
THE GALAXY
2014

FRONTIER

GALAXY QUEST
1999

COWBOY
BEBOP
1997-1998

PROMETHEUS
2012

STAR TREK:
THE NEXT
GENERATION
1987-94

THE FINAL

A L I E N
W A R F A R E

STAR TREK
2009

PITCH BLACK
2000

HITCHHIKER'S
GUIDE TO THE
GALAXY
2005

DOCTOR WHO
1963-89; 2000-
PRESENT

STARSHIP
TROOPERS
1997

SOLARIS
2002

FIREFLY
2002

Dystopias

THESE VISIONS OF THE FUTURE ARE THE END OF THE WORLD AS WE KNOW IT: NOISY, BLEAK, AND ABOVE ALL CHALLENGING

1 The Stand
1978, 1994

The Book of Revelations re-imagined as a mystic-Americana road trip. Stephen King's viral apocalypse bifurcates the citizenry into two distinct societies: a heavenly democratic utopia in progressive Colorado and a sinful demon-fronted hellscape in Las Vegas.

2 The Giver
1993, 2014

Imagine a peaceful community beyond emotion and identity. No one is happy, but no one is sad: Emotion is long since cured. Lois Lowry eschews any futuristic spectacle, painting a portrait of a society that chose the order over chaos.

3 The Hunger Games Trilogy
2008-2015

Welcome to Panem, where the rich are richer, the poor are hopeless, and reality TV is the kid-killing national pastime. Suzanne Collins' climate-catastrophe North America has communist work Districts, a totalitarian despot, and an Orwellian propaganda machine as our dark future.

4 World War Z
2006, 2013

The zombie apocalypse destroys New York, brings peace to the Middle East, and launches an economic Renaissance in Cuba. Max Brooks' novel takes the myth of the walking dead to every sociopolitical extreme.

5 The Road
2006, 2009

The apocalypse to end all apocalypses. Cormac McCarthy's father-son odyssey is a road trip through an impossibly ruined America under a blackened sky. There's nothing left alive—flora

WORLD WAR Z

or fauna—and the only people left alive are the type who eat other people for dinner.

6 12 Monkeys
1995

Viral contamination sends humans underground. Then things start getting weird. From the mind of Terry Gilliam comes a trippy future world where mad scientists cage prisoners in human zoos and send pioneers backward in time.

12 MONKEYS

7 AI: Artificial Intelligence
2001

Manhattan is underwater—and that's by far the least crazy thing about *AI*'s future America, where realistic robo-beings have become the new disenfranchised minority.

8 Terminator 2: Judgment Day
1991

The genius of James Cameron's post-Skynet future—explored considerably in his *Terminator* sequel—is the sheer scope of the artificial intelligence battle-field. The whole planet becomes a World War I battle trench.

9 The Matrix
1999

Machines rule the world, trapping humanity in a digital universe so convincing that most people never even realize they're prisoners. The real world is a bombed-out hopeless wreck. The good news: In the digital world, it's shockingly easy to learn kung fu.

10 Wall-E
2008

Earth is a garbage dump of trash skyscrapers. Humans are immobile couch potatoes. For a kids' movie, *Wall-E* makes some trenchant commentary about our binge-happy modern moment.

11 The Walking Dead
2003-

Robert Kirkman's big idea for a graphic novel—a zombie movie that never ends—became a zeitgeist-defining TV megahit. It's an old-fashioned Western, with gunslinging lead characters building a community in a ruined civilization.

12 Station Eleven
2014

Even when most of the population dies from a pandemic, the survivors will still need their Shakespeare. In Emily St. John Mandel's novel, a troupe of performers travel through post-civilized society, where nations have collapsed into a few villages and towns.

13 The MaddAddam Trilogy
2003-2013

Corporations replace govern-

CONTINUES ON PAGE 150 ▶

DYSTOPIAS CONTINUED FROM PAGE 149

ment. Genetics research creates a new age of bioengineered organisms. The world ends. And then the story begins. Margaret Atwood conjures up a new world that's both a broken-down version of the past and a neo-Edenic future.

14 Mad Max: Fury Road
2015

Director George Miller re-invisioned his postapocalyptic world more than 35 years after his original 1979 film. His magnum opus is a 120-minute chase where steel, death, and fanaticism meet, a movie with almost no dialogue set in a toxic wasteland. It challenges perceptions of women and freedom, heroism and extremism, and perhaps even movies themselves.

15 The Passage and The Twelve
2010-

The as-yet-unfinished trilogy combines several strains of apocalypse chic: viral outbreak, mutant villains, milita-

rized dystopias. But the real joy of Justin Cronin's tale is how post-America America becomes a fantasy landscape of mysterious settlements and unfathomable societies: *The Walking Dead* by way of J.R.R. Tolkien.

16 Zone One
2011

Because after the world ends, someone needs to clean up the mess. *Zone One* by Colson Whitehead begins where most zombie stories end. With order restored, a crew of "sweepers" moves through Manhattan, patiently rekilling the undead. Ironic: The last people left in New York are the exterminators.

17 The Dog Stars
2012

A decade after a humanity-decimating virus, wannabe poet Hig lives a relatively peaceful life in Colorado with his dog and his plane. But he seeks something more.

CONTINUES ON PAGE 152 ▶

Series Finales

SOME OF THESE ENDINGS WERE RIGHT ON TARGET, ELICITING LAUGHS AND GASPS—AND OTHERS WERE SIMPLY HEAD-SCRATCHERS

1	NEWHART	1990
2	SIX FEET UNDER	2005
3	THE SOPRANOS	2007
4	BREAKING BAD	2013
5	BUFFY THE VAMPIRE SLAYER	2003
6	FRIDAY NIGHT LIGHTS	2011
7	THE OFFICE	2013
8	SONS OF ANARCHY	2014
9	PARKS AND RECREATION	2015
10	LOST	2010
11	GLEE	2015
12	PARENTHOOD	2015
13	SEINFELD	1998
14	THE COSBY SHOW	1992
15	CHEERS	1993
16	ROSEANNE	1997
17	MURPHY BROWN	1998
18	HOW I MET YOUR MOTHER	2014
19	FRIENDS	2004
20	SEX AND THE CITY	2004
21	THE WEST WING	2006
22	THE SHIELD	2008
23	BATTLESTAR GALACTICA	2009
24	30 ROCK	2013
25	FRINGE	2013

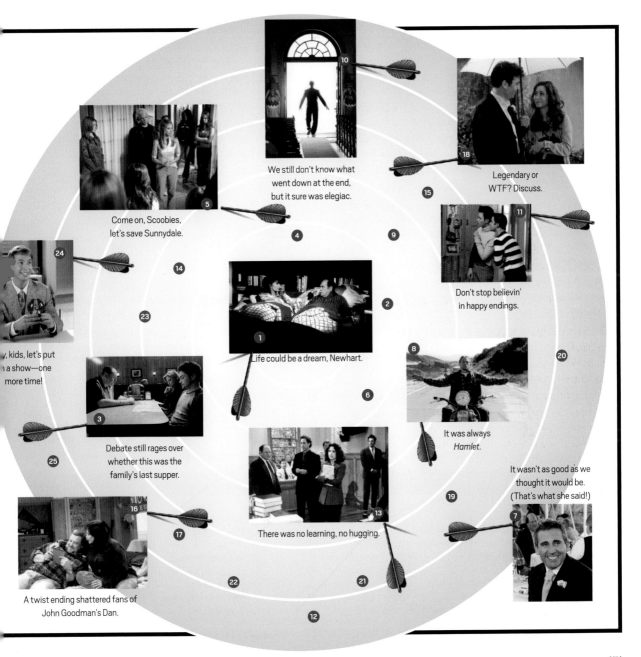

We still don't know what went down at the end, but it sure was elegiac.

Come on, Scoobies, let's save Sunnydale.

Legendary or WTF? Discuss.

Don't stop believin' in happy endings.

kids, let's put a show—one more time!

Life could be a dream, Newhart.

It was always *Hamlet*.

Debate still rages over whether this was the family's last supper.

It wasn't as good as we thought it would be. (That's what she said!)

There was no learning, no hugging.

A twist ending shattered fans of John Goodman's Dan.

Fulfillment. Love? Witness the end of the world as written by Peter Heller as an opportunity for self-actualization.

18 I Am Legend
2007

If there's only one man left on Earth, it might as well be Will Smith. Adapted from Richard Matheson's classic novel, the big-screen *Legend* finds some serenity in a Manhattan reclaimed by nature. Just don't stay out past dark.

19 Snowpiercer
2013

Earth is a frozen ruin. But life persists inside of the Snowpiercer, a perpetual-motion automotive civilization stratified across surreal train cars. When rebels from steerage go questing through Snowpiercer's interior, they find the elite passengers live in extravagant luxury: swimming pools, sushi restaurants, and even a neon-lit nightclub.

20 Children of Men
1992, 2006

Eighteen years after humanity stopped having babies, the United Kingdom is the only government left governing. Most apocalyptic futures are violent, but Alfonso Cuaron's film is a quietly bleak vision of civilization relinquishing itself to oblivion.

21 Contagion
2011

Swine flu, bird flu, SARS: pieces of cake, compared to the invisible outbreak that spreads from Hong Kong throughout the entire world. In Steven Soderbergh's apocalyptic vision, globalization just makes it easier for the whole world to fall together.

22 The Handmaid's Tale
1990

Adapted from Margaret Atwood's pioneering novel, this feminist-tinged future imag-

POP CULTURE OBSESSION

War Movies

TICKET SALES DON'T LIE—WE LOVE TO WATCH THE WORLD BURN. HERE ARE OUR FAVORITES: FROM SPARTA TO THE CIVIL WAR AND BEYOND

1 300
Sparta, Thermopylae, 480 BC.

2 Kingdom of Heaven
Crusaders defending the Kingdom of Jerusalem

3 Braveheart
William Wallace in the First War of Scottish Independance

4 The Last of the Mohicans
The French and Indian War

5 The Patriot
American Revolutionary War

6 Master and Commander: The Far Side of the World
Napoleonic Wars

7 Gettysburg
American Civil War

8 The Last Samurai
Satsuma Revolution

9 Saving Private Ryan
World War II

10 Schindler's List
World War II, Germany

11 Flags of Our Fathers
Battle of Iwo Jima

12 The Pianist
World War II

ines a sterilized, militarized America that forces women to become surrogate concubines.

23 **Falling Skies**
2011-

A powerful army invades America, decimating the population and forcing the survivors into nomadic attack tribes: The fun of TNT's alien apocalypse is how it simultaneously recalls the American Revolution and the native genocide that proceeded it, sending modern-day citizens on their own trail of tears.

24 **The 100**
2014-

A century after the apocalypse, mankind sends 100 teenage criminals back to Earth. It's a new Eden that's also a generation-gap penal colony fraught with native dangers: *Lord of the Flies* meets "Parents Just Don't Understand."

25 **Never Let Me Go**
2005, 2010

At a mysterious boarding school with a special focus on art (and zero focus on anything else), the "students" are actually clones bred for organ donation. Their lives are short, their cloistered world is small, but their love is real. ∎

7   13   21   22   25

1700   4   5   1800   6   7-8   1900   9-16   17   18-21   2000   22-24   2100   2200   25   2300

13 **Downfall**
World War II, Germany

14 **Fury**
World War II, Germany

15 **Inglourious Basterds**
World War II, Germany

16 **The Thin Red Line**
World War II, Battle of Mount Austen

17 **We Were Soldiers**
Vietnam, Battle of Ia Drang

18 **Hotel Rwanda**
Rwandan Civil War

19 **Jarhead**
Operation Desert Storm

20 **Three Kings**
1991 Iraqi Uprising

21 **Black Hawk Down**
Battle of Mogadishu

22 **The Hurt Locker**
Iraq War

23 **American Sniper**
Iraq War

24 **Lone Survivor**
Afghanistan War

25 **Starship Troopers**
Distant future, war with the aliens of Klendathu

It's Been Real

4

Can you remember the real world before *The Real World*? Or life before you carried your album collection in your pocket (on that thing that also makes calls)? As news, technology and fashion becomes entertainment and reality TV makes ordinary folks into stars, we look back at game-changing innovations and true-life stories that kept us riveted.

Reality Stars

IT'S ALL ABOUT MAKING A STRONG IMPRESSION!
THESE ARE THE PERSONALITIES WE LOVED—AND THE
ONES WE LOVED TO HATE

CHRISTIAN SIRIANO

1 Omarosa Manigault
The Apprentice

HATE ——20—— LOVE

Is Omarosa a villain? Or just the perfect capitalist? We can all agree that Omarosa set a new standard for reality amorality, invigorating the genre with a *Game of Thrones* mentality.

2 Christian Siriano
Project Runway

HATE ——50—— LOVE

The youngest *Runway* winner—and the show's best argument for itself—Siriano's legitimate talent was matched only by his talent for catchy one-liners.

3 Richard Hatch
Survivor

HATE ——20—— LOVE

The Great American Reality TV Big Bad. *Survivor*'s first survivor brought the word "alliance" into the lexicon and earned attention for his plotting—and his no-clothes policy.

4 Lauren Conrad
The Hills

HATE ——75—— LOVE

The Laguna Beach everygal spun off on her own big-city adventure, becoming the island-of-sanity Gallant to frenemy Heidi's bad-decision Goofus.

5 Teresa Giudice
The Real Housewives of New Jersey

HATE ——50—— LOVE

Conspicuous consumption personified (and later convicted). The docusoap genre begins and ends with Teresa's table-flip freak-out.

6 Pedro Zamora
The Real World

HATE ——90—— LOVE

American television had never seen his like: a proud gay man living bravely (and openly) with AIDS. Reality TV is still waiting for someone half as real.

7 Dr. Will Kirby
Big Brother

HATE ———————●(70)——— LOVE

An unapologetic cad with a nigh-telepathic gift for gab, Dr. Will defined *Big Brother*'s

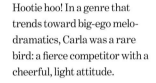

unique strain of mustache-twirling villainy. At least he always stabs in the front.

8 Carla Hall
Top Chef

HATE ——————————●(90) LOVE

Hootie hoo! In a genre that trends toward big-ego melo-dramatics, Carla was a rare bird: a fierce competitor with a cheerful, light attitude.

9 Tyra Banks
America's Next Top Model

HATE ————●(50)———— LOVE

We knew she was a supermodel. But it took *Top Model* to reveal that Tyra was a maniacal space alien sent from the heavens to give young beauties their own Full Metal Jacket.

TYRA
BANKS

10 Uncle Si Robertson
Duck Dynasty

HATE ——————————●(80)— LOVE

Everyone's got that one uncle: the weirdo, the kookbat, the

CONTINUES ON PAGE 158 ▶

Talk Shows that Soared— Or Sank

The Dennis Miller Show	1992	1 YEAR
The Chevy Chase Show	1993	5 WEEKS
The Jon Stewart Show	1993-95	1.5 YEARS
Ricki Lake	1993-2004	10.5 YEARS
Gabrielle (Gabrielle Carteris)	1995-96	1 YEAR
Carnie! (Carnie Wilson)	1995-96	1 YEAR
The Tempestt Bledsoe Show	1995-96	1 YEAR
The Rosie O'Donnell Show	1996-2002	6 YEARS
The Keenen Ivory Wayans Show	1997-98	7 MONTHS
The Chris Rock Show	1997-2000	3.5 YEARS
The Magic Hour (Magic Johnson)	1998	11 EPISODES
The Martin Short Show	1999-2000	1 YEAR
The Queen Latifah Show	1999-2001	2 YEARS
Late World With Zach (Zach Galifianakis)	2002	29 EPISODES
The Caroline Rhea Show	2002-03	1 YEAR
McEnroe (John McEnroe)	2004	1 YEAR
Tyra (Tyra Banks)	2005-10	5 YEARS
The Megan Mullally Show	2006-07	4 MONTHS
The Bonnie Hunt Show	2008-10	2 YEARS
Lopez Tonight (George Lopez)	2009-11	2 YEARS
The Wanda Sykes Show	2009-10	1 YEAR
The Ricki Lake Show	2012-13	1 YEAR
Katie (Katie Couric)	2012-14	2 YEARS
Bethenny (Bethenny Frankel)	2012-14*	2 YEARS
The Queen Latifah Show, take 2	2013-15	2 YEARS

* Including test run in 2012

guy who might be just a little insane. But no way your uncle has a beard half as impressive.

11 Juan Pablo Galavis

The Bachelor

HATE   LOVE
(10)

A sex-idiot supervillain and an emotional terrorist, Juan Pablo set a new standard for mesmerizing narcissism. Have you heard about his daughter?

12 Puck

The Real World

HATE   LOVE
(40)

The sacred requires the profane, so the season of Pedro was also the season of Puck. The snot rockets, the peanut butter: Wouldn't you evict him from your house?

13 Kim Kardashian

Keeping Up With the Kardashians

HATE   LOVE
(60)

Reality TV's greatest creation transformed selfie-age vanity into a boundlessly (and endlessly monetizable) resource. Kim invented a world where her personal life was the brand.

14 Brandi Glanville

The Real Housewives of Beverly Hills

HATE   LOVE
(40)

Her onscreen origin was tragic, but Glanville's ensuing *Housewives* arc is variously infuriating and train-wreck fascinating. Has she found rock bottom?

15 Jonny Fairplay

Survivor

HATE   LOVE
(30)

Sure, Fairplay didn't really play fair. But give the devil his due: The creator of the innovative "Dead Grandmother" strategy was uniquely good at playing bad.

CONTINUES ON PAGE 160 ▶

Reality Shows

HERE ARE THE "UNSCRIPTED" SERIES THAT WERE RIGHT ON TARGET— AND SOME THAT MISSED THE MARK

1	SURVIVOR	2000-PRESENT
2	THE AMAZING RACE	2001-PRESENT
3	THE OSBOURNES	2002-05
4	PROJECT RUNWAY	2004-PRESENT
5	JACKASS	2000-02
6	THE REAL WORLD	1992-PRESENT
7	AMERICAN IDOL	2002-PRESENT
8	TOP CHEF	2006-PRESENT
9	THE APPRENTICE	2004-PRESENT
10	THE VOICE	2011-PRESENT
11	PROJECT GREENLIGHT	2001-03; 2005
12	AMERICA'S NEXT TOP MODEL	2003-04; 2006-PRESENT
13	THE BACHELOR	2002-PRESENT
14	DANCING WITH THE STARS	2005-PRESENT
15	JON & KATE PLUS EIGHT	2007-09
16	THE REAL HOUSEWIVES OF...	2006-PRESENT
17	DEADLIEST CATCH	2005-PRESENT
18	JERSEY SHORE	2009-12
19	THE HILLS	2004-10
20	BANDS ON THE RUN	2001
21	BIG BROTHER	2000-PRESENT
22	BLIND DATE	1999-2006
23	FLAVOR OF LOVE	2006-08
24	KEEPING UP WITH THE KARDASHIANS	2007-PRESENT
25	DUCK DYNASTY	2012-PRESENT

Love him or hate him, he's great TV.

As close as we're going to come to a real-life Addams Family.

Talk about pressure cooking!

And to think they're mothers now

We only have ourselves to blame.

The one competition we'd never vote off the island..

The hairiest show on TV—in more ways than one

It's all about the judges; contestants are never heard from again.

REALITY STARS CONTINUED FROM PAGE 158

J.R. MARTINEZ

16 Kate Gosselin
Jon & Kate Plus 8

HATE ——●50——— LOVE

She was the housewife reimagined as a battalion commander, mothering her children the way Patton marshaled his troops. There followed fame, fortune, divorce, desperation—and *Dancing With the Stars.*

17 NeNe Leakes
The Real Housewives of Atlanta

HATE ——————●70— LOVE

The High Priestess of Telling It Like It Is, NeNe redefined sass into alpha-female heavy artillery. Watching someone argue with her is like watching an ant pick a fight with the God of Thunder.

18 Simon Cowell
American Idol and *The X Factor*

HATE ——●50——— LOVE

They called him acerbic, mean, an elitist Brit picking on try-hard American dreamers. Reality's first great judge told the truth: brutally, hilariously.

19 Nicole Richie
The Simple Life

HATE ——————●70— LOVE

Paris Hilton got the headlines, but her *Simple* sidekick gave the rich-kids-go-country reality-sitcom its goofy, oddly endearing heart.

20 Charla Baklayan Faddoul
The Amazing Race

HATE ———————●85 LOVE

A lovably tough player with enough heart to dominate competitors twice her size.

21 "Boston" Rob Mariano
Survivor

HATE ——————●70— LOVE

Too charming to be a bad guy, too nefarious to be a good guy, the one-time *Survivor* winner is the rascal antihero we deserve.

22 Lisa Vanderpump
The Real Housewives of Beverly Hills

HATE —————●60—— LOVE

The glamorously British SoCal entrepreneur brings trashy class to 90210. She's even more fun on *Vanderpump Rules,* playing a gossipy queen to her beautiful-idiot minions.

23 J.R. Martinez
Dancing With the Stars

HATE ————————●95 LOVE

A wounded Iraq vet who became a motivational speaker, an actor, and one of the most inspiring human beings to ever grace a dance floor.

24 Bethenny Frankel
The Real Housewives of New York

HATE —————●60—— LOVE

She wasn't a housewife. But reality never needed to be real. Her terse sarcasm made her a breakout, but Bethenny's no-bull professionalism infused *Housewives* with Lean-In aspiration.

25 Sam Talbot
Top Chef

HATE ———————●80— LOVE

Talented, beloved by fans, dominant in challenges: Chef Sam was the full package. ■

Musical Competition Shows

THEY FLOODED THE AIRWAVES, TOPPED THE RATINGS, AND OCCASIONALLY CROWNED SINGING SENSATIONS. THESE ARE THE MOMENTS THAT LAUNCHED MILLIONS OF VIRAL VIDEO VIEWS

SANJAYA MALAKAR

AMERICAN IDOL

- **Kelly Clarkson** thrills with "Natural Woman" SEASON 1

- **Phillip Phillips** performs "Home" SEASON 11

- **William Hung** causes a sensation auditioning with "She Bangs" SEASON 3

- **Clay Aiken** sings "Bridge Over Troubled Water" SEASON 2

- **Fantasia Barrino** performs "Summertime" SEASON 3

- **Adam Lambert** sings "Mad World" SEASON 8

- **Steven Tyler** strips and takes a dip SEASON 11

- **Carrie Underwood** performs "Alone" SEASON 4

- **Chris Daughtry** sings "Hemorrhage (In My Hands)" SEASON 5

- **Sanjaya Malakar**'s hair captivates fans SEASON 6

- **Constantine Maroulis** sings "Bohemian Rhapsody" SEASON 4

- **Katharine McPhee** sings "Somewhere Over the Rainbow" SEASON 5

THE VOICE

- **Amanda Brown** sings "Dream On" SEASON 3

- **Josh Kaufman** sings "Stay With Me" SEASON 6

- **"Hallelujah"** An emotional rendition of the song in memory of the Newtown shooting victims SEASON 3

CEELO GREEN

- **Cee Lo Green** sings with Kermit the Frog SEASON 3

- **Juliet Simms** performs "It's a Man's Man's Man's World" SEASON 2

- **Jacquie Lee** sings "I Put a Spell on You" SEASON 5

- **Tessanne Chin** performs "I Have Nothing" SEASON 5

- **Melanie Martinez** sings "Toxic" SEASON 3

THE X FACTOR

- **Jillian Jensen** auditions with an anti-bullying message SEASON 2

- **Britney Spears** can't control her

SUSAN BOYLE

disapproving expressions SEASON 2

BRITAIN'S GOT TALENT

- **Susan Boyle** stuns audition audience with "I Dreamed a Dream" 2009

AMERICA'S GOT TALENT

- **Jackie Evancho,** 10, gets a standing ovation for singing the aria "O mio babbino caro" SEASON 5

- **Michael Grimm** performs "When a Man Loves a Woman" SEASON 5

Comebacks Worth Cheering

TITANIC TALENTS ALL, THEY KNOW THE MEANING OF SECOND
(AND EVEN THIRD) ACTS IN THEIR CAREERS

Timeline: 1990 1992 1993 1994 1995 1996 1997 1998 1999 2000 2001 2002

1 **THOMAS PYNCHON** published his fourth novel, *Vineland*, 17 years after his third

2 **JOHNNY CASH** rejuvenated his career with the album *American Recordings* (1994)

3 **JOHN TRAVOLTA** became cool again in *Pulp Fiction* (1994)

4 **FLEETWOOD MAC** topped the charts with their live reunion album *The Dance* (1997)

5 **DREW BARRYMORE** ended her wild-child period with three starring roles, including *Ever After* (ca. 1998)

6 **TERRENCE MALICK** returned to directing after 20 years with *The Thin Red Line* (1998)

7 **CHER** burned up the charts with "Believe" (1998)

8 **SANTANA** introduced himself to a new generation of fans with his *Supernatural* album (1999)

9 **ROB LOWE** roared back on *The West Wing* (1999)

10 **KYLIE MINOGUE** had the biggest success of her career with "Can't Get You Out of My Head" (2001)

11 **ELLEN DeGENERES**'s acting career stalled when she came out, but her talk show took off (2003)

12 **NEIL PATRICK HARRIS**'s Emmy nominations for *How I Met Your*

20

24

2004 — 2005 — 2006 — 2007 — 2008 — 2009 — 2010 — 2011 — 2012 — 2013 — 2014 — 2015 →

Mother proved Doogie Howser was all grown up (2008-10)

3 **BEN AFFLECK** shook off Bennifer and *Daredevil* with a strong directing debut (2007)

4 **ROBERT DOWNEY JR.** became a blockbuster movie star with *Iron Man* (2008)

5 **JOURNEY**'s new lead singer led to a Top 20 hit and a lucrative tour (ca. 2008)

16 **MICKEY ROURKE** reminded everyone he's a great actor in *The Wrestler* (2008)

17 **JIMMY FALLON** showed off his many talents with a late night show (2009)

18

18 **SADE** hit the big time after a 10-year hiatus with *Soldier of Love* (2010)

19 **CLAIRE DANES** thrilled TV audiences again on *Homeland* (2011)

20 **JESSICA LANGE** scared audiences in *American Horror Story* (2011)

21 **BRITNEY SPEARS** bounced back from tabloid headlines and released *Femme Fatale* (2011)

22 **JARED LETO** returned to acting and netted an Oscar (2013)

23 **MATTHEW McCONAUGHEY** left rom-coms behind and wowed in both film and TV (2013)

24 **GARTH BROOKS** released his first studio album and tour in 13 years (2014)

25 **BJÖRK** shared a cri de coeur about a relationship's end on the powerful *Vulnicura*, her first album in four years (2015)

Fashion Moments

THAT CHANGED ENTERTAINMENT

FROM GLITTER AND GRUNGE TO HAIRCUTS COPIED 'ROUND THE WORLD, THESE WERE POP CULTURE'S COOLEST STYLE HITS

SEX AND THE CITY

with a Gap mock turtleneck, she kick-started the hi-low fashion phenom.

3 Kurt Cobain
1991

The Nirvana frontman became the reluctant king of grunge, inspiring a league of acolytes clad in grandpa cardigans, Converse kicks, and lumberjack plaid.

4 Amy Winehouse
2007

A sweet tart in teeny frocks, bold bras, and sky-high bouffant, the British singer was embraced by high fashion until her personal life took a tragic turn.

1 The Opening Credits of *Sex and the City*
1998

The tutu was just the beginning; Carrie Bradshaw (Sarah Jessica Parker) became the tastemaker who kept on giving. So the next time you wear stilettos to walk the dog, you know who to thank—or blame.

2 Sharon Stone at the Oscars
1996

When the outlandish actress paired Armani and Valentino

5 The Best & Worst Red-Carpet Outfits
2000 and 2001

These days stars are created on the red carpet just as much as they are on screen. Jennifer

JENNIFER
LOPEZ

BJÖRK

Lopez introduced her assets to the world at the 2000 Grammys in a plunging Versace, while Björk's choice of avian apparel at the 2001 Oscars made the Icelandic singer a household name—and a lifelong sartorial punchline.

6 The Rachel
1995

There was no haircut more desired in the Clinton era than the layered shag sported by waitress Rachel Green (Jennifer Aniston) on *Friends*. Twenty years later, Aniston calls it "the ugliest haircut" she's ever seen.

7 Britney Spears
1998

Playing a sexy schoolgirl in "...Baby One More Time" worked music-chart magic for Spears—and set the standard by which all Lolita pop stars are judged.

8 Ally McBeal's Skirts
1997

The hardworking but flighty lawyer (Calista Flockhart) and her much-debated microminis made the workplace a safe haven for women's bare legs everywhere.

CONTINUES ON PAGE 166 ▶

Best Screen Wardrobes

COSTUMES CAN SAY A LOT ABOUT A CHARACTER

	POWERFUL
VEEP	
SCANDAL	
SUITS	
THE GOOD WIFE	
A SINGLE MAN	
THE GREAT GATSBY	
HOUSE OF CARDS	
HANNIBAL	
SEX AND THE CITY	
MAD MEN →	
PRETTY LITTLE LIARS	
GOSSIP GIRL	
THE DEVIL WEARS PRADA	
EMPIRE	
DOWNTON ABBEY	
PRETTY WOMAN	
AMERICAN HUSTLE	
CLUELESS	
MOULIN ROUGE!	
PRISCILLA, QUEEN OF THE DESERT	
CASINO ↗	
THE MINDY PROJECT	
UGLY BETTY	
ROMY AND MICHELE'S HIGH SCHOOL REUNION	
LEGALLY BLONDE	COLORFUL

ALLY McBEAL

THE MATRIX

CLUELESS

9 "Mo Money Mo Problems"

1997
In their coordinated leisure wear, Puff Daddy and Mase elevated bright, baggy tracksuits to hip-hop couture.

10 Courtney Love

1995
The lead singer of Hole stole the crown (or, actually, the tiara) from Aqua Netted beauty queens. She appropriated vintage slip dresses, Mary Janes, and home-grown dye jobs, too. Some said the look played with traditional female stereotypes; others argued it mocked all things girly. The rest of us just thought she rocked.

11 Clueless

1995
Teenagers in designer wares talking endlessly on their cell phones? At the time, it played like an over-the-top parody. Today—oh, whatever.

12 The Matrix

1999
How many leather trenches and Neo-style shades were misguidedly purchased to capture the sleek, futuristic allure of the hit movie? Too many, friends.

13 Marky Mark's Underwear

1991
A.k.a. the waistband that ignited a revolution. The peek-aboo underwear was easy to emulate. The abs, not so much.

14 Fiona Apple

1997
The "Criminal" waif co-opted CK's voyeuristic ads to sell . . . herself—and slippy, strappy tanks—to fans everywhere.

15 André 3000, "Hey Ya!"

2003
The dapper rapper brought body-conscious cuts and quality fabrics to hip-hop's baggier street style.

16 Gwen Stefani

1996
The ska-popster took SoCal street style to the suburbs, popularizing white tanks, studded bra straps, bondage pants, and trackies.

CONTINUES ON PAGE 168 ▶

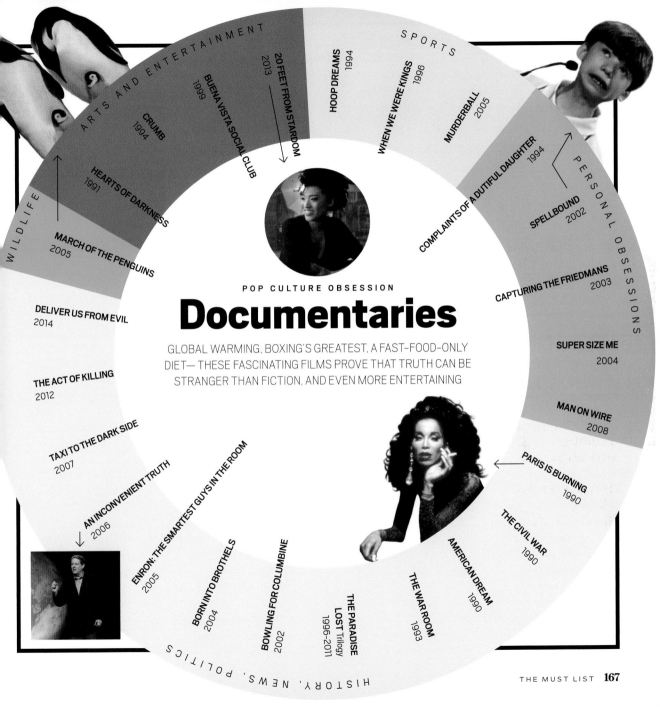

ARTS AND ENTERTAINMENT

SPORTS

20 FEET FROM STARDOM
2013

BUENA VISTA SOCIAL CLUB
1999

CRUMB
1994

HEARTS OF DARKNESS
1991

HOOP DREAMS
1994

WHEN WE WERE KINGS
1996

MURDERBALL
2005

WILDLIFE

MARCH OF THE PENGUINS
2005

POP CULTURE OBSESSION

Documentaries

GLOBAL WARMING, BOXING'S GREATEST, A FAST-FOOD-ONLY
DIET— THESE FASCINATING FILMS PROVE THAT TRUTH CAN BE
STRANGER THAN FICTION, AND EVEN MORE ENTERTAINING

COMPLAINTS OF A DUTIFUL DAUGHTER
1994

PERSONAL OBSESSIONS

SPELLBOUND
2002

CAPTURING THE FRIEDMANS
2003

SUPER SIZE ME
2004

MAN ON WIRE
2008

DELIVER US FROM EVIL
2014

THE ACT OF KILLING
2012

TAXI TO THE DARK SIDE
2007

AN INCONVENIENT TRUTH
2006

ENRON: THE SMARTEST GUYS IN THE ROOM
2005

BORN INTO BROTHELS
2004

BOWLING FOR COLUMBINE
2002

THE PARADISE
LOST Trilogy
1996-2011

THE WAR ROOM
1993

AMERICAN DREAM
1990

THE CIVIL WAR
1990

PARIS IS BURNING
1990

HISTORY, NEWS, POLITICS

FASHION MOMENTS CONTINUED FROM PAGE 166

MARKY MARK

RIHANNA

MADDOX JOLIE-PITT

17 Kanye West
2007

A dedicated follower of both luxury brands and avant-garde outsiders, West inspired a thousand admirers in sunglasses.

18 George Clooney's Caesar
1995

When Dr. Doug Ross cut his curly locks on *ER*, he sparked a hair craze for the male masses—and rolled out Clooney 2.0, debonair movie star.

19 The Strokes
2001

Why are entire cities filled with hipsters wearing blazers, rocker tees, and skinny jeans? Blame this band.

20 Rihanna
2007

Many an R&B diva has taken on big-name fashion before, but none with the saucy punk-rock spirit of the Barbados-born songstress. She started out demure, but in chopping her locks she carved out her own identity—and a bob that was widely copied.

21 Maddox's Fauxhawk
2004

When the little guy surfaced at mom Angelina's premiere with a spiky blue 'do, he set off a trend of adult-size 'hawks—and designer babies.

22 Shania's Midriff
1995

Nashville roared with disapproval at the sight of the crooner's bare belly—until Twain topped the charts. Now sultry country honeys abound.

Athletes and Musicians Who Caught the Acting Bug

THEY STARRED IN TV EPISODES, MOVIES, LATE NIGHT, AND MORE

Justin Timberlake	24 →
Will Smith	177
Madonna	22
Tim McGraw	10
Mark Wahlberg	43
LL Cool J	252
Beyoncé	12
Jennifer Hudson	16 →
Harry Connick Jr.	49
Dwayne Johnson	49
Common	55
Jon Bon Jovi	26
Lenny Kravitz	8
Queen Latifah	178
Ice-T	421
Björk	5
Ice Cube	55
Shaquille O'Neal	25
Terry Bradshaw	17
Michael Jordan	3
Dennis Rodman	27
Courtney Love	22 →
Mike Tyson	31
Lawrence Taylor	12
Vinnie Jones	85

*MOVIES AND TV EPISODES ACTED IN

90210

23 Seth Cohen's Geek Chic

2003

Ushering in the age of the Penguin-attired nerd, Adam Brody turned his dorky alter ego into *The O.C.*'s unexpected cool kid.

24 Ashton's Trucker Hats

2003

Could the *Punk'd* maestro's biggest prank have been getting legions of hipsters to adopt the mesh-and-foam chapeaus of their fathers?

25 The *90210* 'Burns

1990

Now everyone knows size matters ... when it comes to sideburns. The first TV teen drama of the '90s gave teen mags a new crop of cover boys and increased sideburn length by 56 percent. ∎

Award-Show

MOMENTS

WHEN A SHOW IS LIVE
(OR EVEN ON A SEVEN-
SECOND DELAY), ALMOST
ANYTHING CAN HAPPEN,
AS THESE INDELIBLE
INSTANCES PROVED!

1 Madonna, Britney Spears, and Christina Aguilera

kiss at the 2003 VMAs

Two generations of pop divas
come together in a trashy-
delightful lesbian-chic ménage.
Scandalous cherry on top: The
original broadcast featured a
well-timed audience cut to
Britney's ex Justin Timberlake.

2 Britney

performs with the albino
python, 2001 VMAs

At the turn of the millennium,
Britney Spears simply was
MTV. One year after stripping
to the Rolling Stones'
"Satisfaction," she returned
with her most gloriously
shameless VMA display: "I'm
a Slave 4 U," performed with

BRITNEY
SPEARS

KANYE WEST,
TAYLOR SWIFT

an extraordinarily unsubtle python.

3 Kanye
interrupts Taylor Swift at the podium, 2009 VMAs

Yo, Taylor. We're really happy for you, and we're gonna let you finish, but Kanye West interrupting your VMA acceptance speech was the best interruption of all time. Of all time!

4 Adrien Brody
goes in for a sloppy kiss with Halle Berry, 2002 Oscars

Brody stunned everyone when he beat out Jack Nicholson, Daniel Day-Lewis, and Michael Caine to become the youngest Best Actor winner ever. Then he literally swept Halle Berry off her feet. It could only be all downhill from there.

5 Woody Allen
makes his only appearance at the Oscars, post-911 in 2002

No matter how many Oscar nominations the Academy showered on Allen's films, the filmmaker always avoided the ceremony. But post-9/11, a year in which he had no film

CONTINUES ON PAGE 173 ▶

Best Memoirs

STIRRING STORIES OF LIVES WELL-LIVED

William Styron	DARKNESS VISIBLE	1990
Jung Chang	WILD SWANS	1991
Art Spiegelman	MAUS , PARTS I & II	1993
Lucy Grealy	AUTOBIOGRAPHY OF A FACE	1994
Mary Karr	THE LIARS' CLUB	1995
Frank McCourt	ANGELA'S ASHES	1996
Caroline Knapp	DRINKING: A LOVE STORY	1996
Ruth Reichl	TENDER AT THE BONE	1998
Paula Fox	BORROWED FINERY	2001
Alexandra Fuller	DON'T LET'S GO TO THE DOGS TONIGHT	2001
James Frey	A MILLION LITTLE PIECES	2003
Craig Thompson	BLANKETS	2003
Jeannette Walls	THE GLASS CASTLE	2005
Joan Didion	THE YEAR OF MAGICAL THINKING	2005
Alison Bechdel	FUN HOME	2006
Cupcake Brown	A PIECE OF CAKE	2006
Shalom Auslander	FORESKIN'S LAMENT	2007
Ishmael Beah	A LONG WAY GONE: MEMOIRS OF A BOY SOLDIER	2007
David Carr	THE NIGHT OF THE GUN	2008
Patti Smith	JUST KIDS	2010
Caitlin Moran	HOW TO BE A WOMAN	2011
Cheryl Strayed	WILD	2012
Marcus Samuelsson	YES, CHEF	2012
Jeanette Winterson	WHY BE HAPPY WHEN YOU COULD BE NORMAL?	2012
Sonali Deraniyagala	WAVE	2013

Must-See News Events

YES, KIDS, THERE WERE TIMES BEFORE TWITTER WHEN PEOPLE GATHERED TO WATCH AND COMMENT ON BREAKING NEWS. HERE ARE 25 EVENTS THAT DEMANDED IMMEDIATE ATTENTION

- **Anita Hill** harassment testimony at Clarence Thomas' Supreme Court confirmation hearings (OCT 1991)

- **The Clintons** deny his affair with Gennifer Flowers on *60 Minutes* (JAN 1992)

- Riots break out in L.A. after the **Rodney King** verdict (LATE APR–EARLY MAY 1992)

- **Johnny Carson**'s last *Tonight Show* (MAY 22, 1992)

- **Oprah** interviews **Michael Jackson** at the Neverland Ranch (FEB 1993)

- The slow-speed chase of **O.J. Simpson**'s white Bronco (JUNE 1994)

- **Hugh Grant** answers **Jay Leno**'s question about Divine Brown, "What the hell were you

O.J. SIMPSON

THE CLINTONS

HUDSON PLANE LANDING

thinking?" on *The Tonight Show* (JULY 1995)

- **Christopher Reeve**'s first interview after his accident, with **Barbara Walters** (SEPT 1995)

- **O.J. Simpson** is found not guilty of murder (OCT 1995)

- **Princess Diana**'s funeral (SEPT 1997)

- 70 million viewers watch **Barbara Walters** interview **Monica Lewinsky** (1999)

- The countdown to **New Year's Eve 2000** amid Y2K concerns (DEC 31, 1999)

- **Election night 2000**, when no winner was declared (NOV 2000)

- The emotional first *SNL* show after 9/11 (SEPT 29, 2001)

- 22 million watch **Kelly Clarkson** become the first American Idol (SEPT 2002)

- **Whitney Houston** tells **Diane Sawyer** "Crack is wack" (DEC 2002)

- **Oprah** eviscerates **James Frey** for fabricating parts of *A Million Little Pieces* (2006)

- **Katie Couric**'s unexpectedly revealing **Sarah Palin** interviews (2008)

- **Chesley "Sully" Sullenberger**'s miracle plane landing on the Hudson (JAN 15, 2009)

- **President Obama**'s first inauguration (JAN 20, 2009)

- **Prince William and Kate Middleton**'s royal wedding (APR 2011)

SARAH PALIN KATIE COURIC

- **Casey Anthony** found not guilty of murder (JULY 2011)

- **Lance Armstrong** admits to Oprah that he doped (JAN 2013)

- **Manhunt in Boston** for the marathon bombers (APR 2013)

- **Diane Sawyer** interviews **Bruce Jenner** about his transition (APR 2015)

BRUCE JENNER

JACK PALANCE

to promote, he came on stage for a moving tribute to New York cinema, thanking Hollywood for its support.

6 Michael Jackson
kisses wife Lisa Marie Presley, 1994 VMAs
Jackson walked on stage holding his new bride's hand. "Just think," he said, "nobody thought this would last." It did not.

7 Aretha Franklin
sings opera, filling in for Pavarotti, 1998 Grammys
Every now and then, one of the world's greatest opera singers cancels an appearance at the last minute. And every now and then, the undisputed Queen of Soul agrees to fill in for him.

8 Jack Palance
does one-armed push-ups, 1991 Oscars
The 73-year-old Hollywood lifer gave the most exuberant Oscar speech ever: After winning Best Supporting Actor for *City Slickers*, he performed three one-armed push-ups on stage. "As far as the two-handed push-ups are concerned," he said, "you can do that all night."

9 Roberto Benigni
climbs over people's seats to reach the podium, 1998 Oscars
Yes, Roberto Benigni won two awards in a single night. More impressive: He remains the only person in history to celebrate his first Oscar win by jumping on the back of Steven Spielberg's chair.

10 Ellen DeGeneres
organizes Oscars selfie, 2014 Oscars
The perfect snapshot microcosm of a whole era in Hollywood history. It quite literally overloaded Twitter

CONTINUES ON PAGE 175 ▶

ELLEN DeGENERES' OSCAR SELFIE

Oprah Winfrey

SHE CHANGED THE FACE OF DAYTIME TV AND INJECTED NEW LIFE INTO BOOK PUBLISHING. IF ANYONE DESERVES TO BE A BILLIONAIRE, IT'S OPRAH

PRIMETIME EMMY

4 / 1

NOMINATIONS / WIN

DAYTIME EMMY

26 / 18

NOMINATIONS / WINS

3

age when she learned to read

74

selections made for Oprah's Book Club since 1996

19

age when she became the youngest person and first African-American woman to anchor the news at Nashville's WTVF-TV

2

Oscar nominations she's received (for Best Supporting Actress in *The Color Purple* and for *Selma* as Best Picture)

8

times she's appeared on *Time*'s 100 Most Influential People in the World list

28,000

approximate number of guests on her talk show over 25 seasons

FIVE

U.S. presidents who appeared on the show

27

appearances on the show by Celine Dion, the most frequent female guest (other than Oprah's BFF, Gayle King)

25

appearances on the show by Chris Rock, the most frequent male guest (after regulars Dr. Phil, Dr. Oz, and Nate Berkus)

40 MILLION+

viewers of her show per week in the U.S.

20 MILLION+

letters received by the show via U.S. mail over 25 seasons

276

Pontiac G6s given out to audience members on the 2004 season premiere

1998

year she appeared on the cover of *Vogue*

$3 BILLION

her estimated net worth

$12 MILLION

donation she made in 2013 to the Smithsonian's National Museum of African American History and Culture (just one instance of her philanthropy)

29

years she's been with her love, Stedman Graham

51

age she was when she got her ears pierced, on her show

67

pounds of fat she wheeled onto her show in 1988, representing weight she'd lost

4:29:15 time she finished running the Marine Corps Marathon in 1994

1993

year President Clinton signed into law the National Child Protection Act, a.k.a. the "Oprah Bill," creating a database to track child abusers

28 MILLION

Twitter followers

2000

year she launched *O, The Oprah Magazine*

2011

year she launched OWN: the Oprah Winfrey Network

CONTINUED FROM PAGE 173

with the number of retweets. Also, proof that Bradley Cooper is very good at framing.

11 Diana Ross
goes hands-on with Lil' Kim's pastie, 1999 VMAs

That time Diana Ross was greeted by a small rapper in a revealing sparkly purple bodysuit, and Mary J. Blige looked on, her expression unreadable.

12 Lady Gaga
wears meat dress, 2010 VMAs

Gaga's rise to fame turned into a game of fashion brinkmanship, with the ascendant diva constantly topping herself for weirdo style. The grotesque high point: the meat dress, complete with an uncooked-meat cap.

13 Lady Gaga
(again!) stuns with *Sound of Music* songs, 2014 Oscars

LADY GAGA

A half-decade on from butcher-chic, Gaga confirmed her newfound mature phase with a musical medley honoring *The Sound of Music*. A visibly delighted Julie Andrews appeared on stage to bless her with a hug.

14 Beyoncé
reveals her baby bump, 2011 VMAs

Beyoncé is the trendiest of Trending Topics. But the undisputed champion of Internet-breaking events

CONTINUES ON PAGE 176 ▶

MELISSA ETHERIDGE

confirmed Etheridge as one of music's bravest, most unapologetic performers.

16 Van Halen

reunites for the first time in a decade, 1996 VMAs

"This is the first time that we've actually stood on stage together in over a decade," declared singer David Lee Roth, reunited ever-so-briefly with his fellow band members. And Roth's attention hogging ensured they'd never all be on stage together again.

17 Robin Thicke

gets creepy and Miley Cyrus twerks, 2013 VMAs

Briefly popular thanks to douche anthem "Blurred Lines," Thicke walked on stage for his big moment wearing a supervillain striped suit. He immediately got twerked right out of the zeitgeist by Cyrus, wearing a suggestive foam finger (and not much else.)

18 Britney Spears

mounts bloated,

unsuccessful "comeback," 2007 VMAs

What does it look like when a whole pop culture era ends? For Britney Spears—in a grueling breakdown year of

heavily publicized hospitalizations, court visits, and head-shaving—it looks like three minutes of awkward gyrations and bad lip-synching.

ROBIN THICKE, MILEY CYRUS

outdid herself when she ended her "Love on Top" number with official bun-in-the-oven confirmation. Earth, meet Blue Ivy.

15 Melissa Etheridge

makes first appearance with bald head while fighting cancer, 2005 Grammys

Coming off a round of chemotherapy for breast cancer, the singer-songwriter duetted on "Piece of My Heart" in tribute to Janis Joplin. The song became a cancer-battle anthem—and once again

19 Jennifer Lawrence

trips on her way to the podium, 2013 Oscars

A perfect moment: Ascendant young superstarlet crowns a big year with the big prize. A minor calamity: The starlet falls on the steps. An even more perfect moment: She picks herself up, not even noticing that Hugh Jackman and Bradley Cooper—two Sexiest Men Alive!—are running to her aid.

20 David Letterman

cracks painful "Uma . . . Oprah . . ." joke, 1994 Oscars

Letterman's Oscar-hosting gig isn't as bad as you remember—except for his opening Uma Thurman/Oprah Winfrey riff, a dead-air gag that became the go-to example of award-show train-wreck hosting.

21 Jodie Foster

comes out, 2013 Golden Globes

The famously private Foster gave a teasingly circuitous speech about herself and Hollywood. While she "came out," she also deconstructed what it means to come out—and the idea of privacy in a time when every celebrity has "a press conference, a fragrance, and a prime-time reality show."

22 Jennifer Hudson

performs emotional "You Pulled Me Through" after murders of her mother, brother, and nephew, 2008 Grammys

Mere months after the devastating shooting deaths of her mother, brother, and nephew, the *Idol* breakout-turned-Oscar winner delivered an impossibly touching performance on stage. (She won her first Grammy that night.)

23 John Travolta

muffs Idina Menzel's name, 2014 Oscars

Oh, the unplanned joys of live television! We expect the unexpected—accidental f-bombs, political demonstrations, wardrobe malfunctions. But when the *Pulp Fiction* star introduced the *Frozen* songstress as "Adele Dazeem," he raised the act of flubbing into a Twitter-imploding art form.

BOB DYLAN, MICHAEL PORTNOY

24 Bob Dylan

gets Soy Bomb-ed, 1998 Grammys

Dylan was pleasantly singing "Love Sick," a song so inoffensive that Victoria's Secret turned it into an ad. Then performance artist Michael Portnoy ran up next to Dylan, "Soy Bomb" scrawled across his bare chest. Gesticulating (and gate-crashing TV history) ensued.

25 Christopher Reeve

appears in a wheelchair to introduce films clips about social issues, 1995 Oscars

Less than a year after an accident left him paralyzed from the neck down, the once and future Superman appeared on stage. The standing ovation lasted a full minute. Then he started talking—and had to keep pausing for more applause. ∎

Tech Innovations

THAT CHANGED ENTERTAINMENT

IN WHICH WE PAY TRIBUTE TO THE GROUNDBREAKING WAYS ENTERTAINMENT GETS CREATED AND CONSUMED

1 The DVD Player
1997

The living room was never the same after home movie-viewing went digital. Within five years, 31 million couch potatoes shelled out for the device that conjured vivid visuals from nifty little discs. At the time, it was the fastest adoption rate of any new consumer-electronics product—ever.

2 iTunes Music Store
2003

While it wasn't the first MP3 hub, it was the one that rocked the music world and legitimized paying for singles. The entertainment industry is still reeling.

3 TiVo
1999

One of the first digital video recorders, it finally put an end to the days when all television junkies were held hostage to the networks'

LAWNMOWER MAN

scheduling whims (or clunky VCR timers).

4 iPod
2001
First Apple gave us a cool portable gadget to play downloaded music. Then in '03, the company gave us the iTunes Store, a legal way to fill it.

5 YouTube
2005
How did we ever live without the immediate gratification of streaming clips featuring funny cats and weeping Britney Spears fans?

6 Realistic CG Characters
1991
Movie directors have used computer-generated graphics to spice up their work since the '70s. But *Terminator 2*'s mercury-morphing assassin blew everyone away with an awesome new blend of human acting and digital imagery.

7 Consumer-Friendly Digital Video Cameras
1995
Once available to the public, these gizmos revolutionized filmmaking, enabling us to embrace our inner DeMille on the cheap.

8 Flat-Panel TVs
1997
Stylish and thin, but not vapid: These wonders would go on to popularize high-def TV.

9 Facebook
2004
With more than 1.4 billion active profiles, this social-networking site has created superstars and viral posts aplenty and added to the English language (vague-booking, anyone?).

10 Stadium Seating in Multiplexes
1995
Here's to being able to watch a movie without craning your neck to see around that bouffant three rows ahead.

11 Smarterphones
2007
Now that we have the Internet in our pocket (thank you, Apple), any bar argument can be quickly settled by Google, we'll never be lost, and selfies taken in the 2010s will all have an Instagram filter.

12 Netscape Navigator
1994
Surfing the Web was a mere pipe dream before the advent of this pioneering Internet browser.

13 PlayStation 2
2000
Sony's sleek model redefined the gaming experience with superior graphics and the

CONTINUES ON PAGE 180 ▶

estimated number of books available on Amazon **3.4 MILLION**

BULLET
TIME

Maybe the book won't die after all—it'll just be displaced. Amazon.com's Kindle, a handheld device that lets you download and read book-length texts, was already a success after less than a year.

19 Bullet Time
1999
Effects master John Gaeta's slowed-down, rotating action sequences for *The Matrix* popularized this mind-blowing camera style. Keanu Reeves said it best: "Whoa."

20 Auto-Tune
1997
The music-processing software that made Paris Hilton palatable to your ears—a mixed blessing, indeed.

21 Twitter
2006
Who knew 140 characters could be so powerful? The microblogging site started as a way to share what you're eating and ended as a tool used by revolutionaries to topple regimes.

ability to read DVDs. Within five years, it had sold a staggering 100 million units worldwide.

14 Netflix
1998
Why trek to the store when movies can come to you by mail? That idea—so simple, yet so ruthless—shattered the booming brick-and-mortar rental business and continued to do so when Instant Streaming debuted. Netflix is responsible for nearly a third of all downstream Web traffic in North America.

15 Body Motion Capture
1992
The Lawnmower Man redefined an old trick: recording a human actor's movements in a sensor-covered suit. Nine years later, *The Lord of the Rings* advanced the technique to transform Andy Serkis into the unforgettable Gollum.

16 Amazon.com
1995
Launched to sell the lowest-tech entertainment—books—

the site has mushroomed into one of the most influential online megastores.

17 Polyphonic Ringtones
2002
Whether your taste runs to Soulja Boy or Stravinsky, this wildly profitable innovation has helped personalize cell phones and usher them into the multimedia world.

18 The Amazon Kindle
2007

22 **Spotify**
2008

By 2015, the online music, podcast, and video-streaming service had over 75 million users and kicks back 70% of its total revenue to artists for royalties.

23 **Nintendo Wii**
2006

The Wii Remote controller detects movement, allowing players to manipulate their Miis by physical action. Over 900 million Wii games have been sold to date.

24 **Twitch**
2011

The live-streaming service turned videogaming into a spectator sport and by 2015 reported 100 million visitors per month.

25 **Selfie Sticks**
2011

TIME magazine named the Narcisstick one of the Top 25 inventions of the year in 2014, and they quickly became annoying at concerts everywhere. ■

Biggest Movie Bombs

MOVIE		TOTAL COST	• NET LOSS	• EARNINGS
2011	*Mars Needs Moms*	$150 MILL	–$111 MIL	$39 MILL
1999	*The 13th Warrior*	$160 MILL	–$98.3 MIL	$61.7 MM
2002	*The Adventures of Pluto Nash*	$100 MILL	–$92.9 MIL	$7.1 MILL
2004	*The Alamo*	$107 MILL	–$81.2 MIL	$25.8 MILL
2001	*Town & Country*	$90 MILL	–$79.6 MIL	$10.4 MILL
2001	*Supernova*	$90 MILL	–$75.2 MIL	$14.8 MILL
2010	*The Nutcracker in 3D*	$90 MILL	–$73.8 MIL	16.2 MILL
2010	*How Do You Know*	$120 MILL	–$71.3 MIL	$48.7 MILL
1995	*Cutthroat Island*	$98 MILL	–$69.5 MILL	$18.5 MILL
2005	*The Great Raid*	$80 MILL	–$69.2 MIL	$10.8 MILL
2005	*A Sound of Thunder*	$80 MILL	–$68.3 MIL	$11.7 MILL
2001	*Monkeybone*	$75 MILL	–$67.4 MIL	$7.6 MILL
1997	*The Postman*	$80 MILL	–$62.4 MIL	$17.6 MILL
2001	*Osmosis Jones*	$75 MILL	–$61 MIL	$14 MILL
1997	*Lolita*	$62 MILL	–$60.9 MIL	$1.1 MILL
1999	*Dudley Do-Right*	$70 MILL	–$60.1 MIL	$9.9 MILL
2005	*Stealth*	$135 MILL	–$58 MIL	$77 MILL
1999	*Chill Factor*	$70 MILL	–$58 MIL	$12 MILL
1998	*Beloved*	$80 MILL	–$57 MIL	$23 MILL
1999	*The Astronaut's Wife*	$75 MILL	–$55.4 MIL	$19.6 MILL
2001	*Final Fantasy: The Spirits Within*	$137 MILL	–$51.9 MIL	$85.1 MILL
2002	*Ballistic: Ecks vs. Sever*	$70 MILL	–$50.1 MIL	$19.9 MILL
1991	*Hudson Hawk*	$65 MILL	–$47.8 MIL	$17.2 MILL
2000	*Red Planet*	$80 MILL	–$46.6 MIL	$33.4 MILL
1998	*Soldier*	$60 MILL	–$45 MIL	$15 MILL

*COSTS ARE ESTIMATES; GROSSES ARE BASED ON GLOBAL BOX OFFICE; THE MOVIES ARE RANKED ACCORDING TO THEIR NET LOSSES, ADJUSTED FOR INFLATION

Index

Photo Credits

Front Cover
Downey Jr., Schwarzenegger, Hanks, Hamilton: Zade Rosenthal (4); Knowles: Parkwood Entertainment; Gleeson: Helen Sloan/HBO; Cast Away: Francois Duhamel; Murray: Louis Goldman; Silverstone: Elliott Marks; Colbert: Comedy Central; Winfrey: Art Streiber/OWN; Tennant: Adrian Rogers/BBC; Toy Story: © Disney/Pixar; Rowling: Debra Hurford Brown; Laurie: Jordin Althaus/FOX; Gellar: Andrew MacPherson/WB; Washington: Craig Sjodin/ABC; Anderson: Michael Lavine/FOX; Radcliffe: Peter Mountain; Gandolfini: Barry Wetcher/HBO; Lawrence: Tim Palen; Astin: Pierre Vinet/HBO; Bale: Stephen Vaughan; Cumberbatch: Robert Viglasky/Hartswood Films for Masterpiece; Pike: Merrick Morton; Esposito: Ursula Coyote/AMC; Romijn: Attila Dory; Paul, Cranston: Frank Ockenfels 3/AMC (2); Aniston: Andrew Eccles/NBC; Kaling: Emily Shur/FOX; Depp: Anthony Mandler; Scott: Nick Wall/HBO; C.K.: Frank Ockenfels/FX; Pratt: © Marvel 2014; Parker: Mark Liddell/HBO; Gyllenhaal: Kimberly French; Sheen: James Sorensen/NBC; Clarke: HBO; Smith: Nick Briggs/PBS; Roberts: Ron Batzdorff; Lange: Robert Zuckerman/FX; Garner: Sheryl Nields/ABC; The Lion King: © Disney; Damon: George Kraychyk; Leakes: Alex Martinez/Bravo; Reedus: Gene Page/AMC; Jackman: James Fisher; McDormand: Michael Tackett; Le Blanc: NBC; Sagal: Ray Mickshaw/FX; Kardashian: Anders Overgaard/E!;Leto:

Anne Marie Fox; Myers: Kimberly Wright; Jackson: Linda R. Chen; Fey: Art Streiber/NBC; Trump: Patrick Randak/NBC; SpongeBob SquarePants: Nickelodeon; Redmayne: Liam Daniel.

Back Cover
Streep: Brigitte Lacombe; Elba: Steven Neaves/BBC; Davis, Nixon: Mark Liddell/HBO (2); South Park, Stewart: Comedy Central (2); Hall: HBO; King: Shane Leonard; Poehler, Offerman: Chris Haston/NBC (2); Reeves: Melinda Sue Gordon; Woody: © Disney/Pixar; Henson, Duchovny: Michael Lavine/FOX (2); Astin: Pierre Vinet; Paquin: John P. Johnson/HBO; Adele: Andrew Yee; Moyer: Steven Lippman/HBO; Williams: Nicole Rivellli/HBO; Bell: Mike Ansell/CW; Shrek: © Dreamworks (2); Travolta: Linda R. Chen; Pattinson: Kimberley French; Pompeo: Randy Holmes/ABC; Baldwin: Art Streiber/NBC; Schumer: Peter Yang/Comedy Central; Frozen: © Disney; Wilson: Mitchell Haaseth/NBC; Gurira, Reedus: Gene Page/AMC (2); Minions: Universal Pictures/Illumination Entertainment; Perry: Michael Grecco/FOX; Smith: Barry Wetcher; Mirren: PBS; Pratt: © Marvel 2014; Lawrence: Tim Palen; Wallis: Jess Pinkham; Thurman: Andrew Cooper; Harris: Ron P. Jaffe/CBS; Polizzi: MTV; Hunnam: Michael Becker/FX; Archer: FX; Louis-Dreyfus: Patrick Harbron/HBO; Fallon: James White/NBC; Spelling: Diego Uchitel/FOX; The Lego Movie: Courtesy of Warner Bros.

Chapter 1
Introduction: P 4, Lori Stoll/Retna; P 6, Knowles: Parkwood Entertainment; Gandolfini: Barry Wetcher/HBO; Rowling: Debra Hurford Brown; Cranston: Frank Ockenfels 3/AMC; McDormand: Michael Tackett; Murray: Louis Goldman; Aniston: Andrew Eccles/NBC; Gellar: Andrew MacPherson/WB; **The Greats Movies**: P 8-9, Pulp Fiction: Miramax/Buena Vista/Kobal Collection; Saving Private Ryan: David James; The Silence of the Lambs: Ken Regan/Camera 5; Toy Story: © Pixar/Disney; P 10-11, Edward Scissorhands: Zade Rosenthal; 12 Years A Slave: Francois Duhamel; Dances With Wolves: Ben Glass; Birdman: Atsushi Nishijima; P 12-13, Hanks: Spencer Heyfron/Redux; Oscar statuette: Albert Watson/Oscar (r) Statuette © A.M.P.A.S. (r); Cast Away: Francois Duhamel; asteroid: Universal History Archive/UIG via Getty Images; Joe Versus the Volcano: Warner Bros/Everett Collection; Sleepless In Seattle: TriStar/Everett Collection; You've Got Mail: Brian Hamill; Forest Gump: Paramount/Kobal Collection; Rushmore: Touchstone/Kobal Collection; P 14-15, Shrek: DreamWorks Animation SKG; Fight Club: Merrick Morton; A Few Good Men: Columbia/Photofest; **The Greats Comedies**: P 16-17, Office Space: Van Redin; There's Something About Mary: Glenn Watson; Braveheart: 20th Century Fox/Everett Collection; Elizabeth: Everett Collection; Lincoln: David James; La Vie en Rose: Bruno Calvo; The Aviator: Andrew Cooper; Beautiful Mind: Eli

Reed; Ali: Frank Connor; What's Love Got to Do With It: Buena Vista/Everett Collection; Dead Man Walking: Gramercy Pictures/Everett Collection; P 18-19, 40-Year-Old Virgin: Suzanne Hanover; Y Tu Mama Tambien: Daniel Daza; The Celebration: Nimbus Film/Kobal Collection; Leviathan: Anna Matveeva; Il Postino: Mary Evans/Everett Collection; Tsotsi: Blid Alsbirk; A Separation: Habib Madjidi; Crouching Tiger, Hidden Dragon: Chan Kam Chuen; P 20-21, Murray: Karina Taira/Contour by Getty Images; Anderson: Philippe Antonello; Ramis: Columbia/Everett Collection; Murray (golfing): Jeff Gross/Getty Images; Lost in Translation: Yoshio Sato; Groundhog Day: Columbia/Photofest; Where the Buffalo Roam: Everett Collection; Hyde Park On Hudson: Nicola Dove; P 22-23, Election: Bob Akester; Napoleon Dynamite: Aaron Ruell; Dicaprio: Samir Hussein/WireImage; P 24-25, Cool Runnings: Buena Vista/Photofest; Million Dollar Baby: Merie W. Wallace; Rudy: Van Redin; Best in Show: Doane Gregory/Warner Bros/Kobal Collection; P 26-27, Tree of Life: Cottonwood Pictures/Kobal Collection; The Secret Life of Walter Mitty: 20th Century Fox/Everett Collection; Before Midnight: Despina Spyrou; Lost in Translation: Yoshio Sato; The Motorcycle Diaries: Focus Films/Everett Collection; The Adventures of Priscilla, Queen of The Desert: E. Lockwood/Polygram/Kobal Collection; **The Greats Television**: P 28-29 The Simpsons: FOX; The X-Files: 20th Century Fox/Everett

Collection; Hannibal: Brooke Palmer/NBC; Seinfeld: George Lange/NBC/The Kobal Collection; Entourage: Claudette Barius/HBO; P 30-31, The Office: BBC; Buffy the Vampire Slayer: Frank Ockenfels3/WB; Lost: Mario Perez/ABC; P 33, Beverly Hills 90210: FOX; Fresh Prince of Bel Air: NBC/Everett Collection; P 34-35, The Larry Sanders Show: Larry Watson/HBO; Broadchurch: Patrick Redmond/ITV; Top Gear: Grant Wardrop/BBC; Doctor Who: Adrian Rogers/BBC (2); Luther: Robert Viglasky/BBC; Sherlock: Colin Hutton/Hartswood Films/BBC; Graham Norton, Life on Mars: BBC (2); Absolutely Fabulous, Coupling: BBC/Everett Collection (2); Call the Midwife: Laurence Cendrowicz/PBS; Downton Abbey: Carnival Film & Television Limited 2012 for Masterpiece; Extras: Ray Burmiston/HBO; **The Greats Cult TV**: P 36-37, Buffy the Vampire Slayer: Richard Cartwright/WB; The Comeback: Bruce Birmelin/The Sundance Channel; P 38-39, My So-Called Life: ABC/Kobal Collection; Battlestar Galactica: Paul Michaud/Syfy; P 40-41, Cranston: Mike McGregor/Contour by Getty Images; Emmy statuette: Getty Images; Bee: Antagain/Getty Images; From the Earth to the Moon: HBO/Everett Collection; Peanuts: StockFood/Getty Images; P 43, Archer: FX; House: Michael Yarish/FOX; **The Greats Albums**: P 44-45, Hill: Anthony Barboza/Getty Images; A Tribe Called Quest: Michael Benabib/Retna; U2: Mauro Carraro/Sygma/Corbis; P 46-47, Yeezy sneakers: Amanda Edwards/WireImage;

West and Swift: Jason DeGrow/AP Images; Yeezus tour: R. Chiang/Splash News/Corbis; Cobain: Frank Micelotta/Getty Images; P 48-49, Wayne's World: Paramount/Photofest; First Wives Club: Paramount/Everett Collection; Boogie Nights: New Line/Photofest; The Royal Tenenbaums: James Hamilton/Touchstone/Kobal Collection; Beyonce: Robin Harper/Invision/AP Images; P 50-51, Psy: MediaPunch/Rex USA; White Stripes: Kevin Westenberg/Contour by Getty Images; Adele: Andrew Yee; Ross: Frank Micelotta/Getty Images; **The Greats Videos**: P 52-53, Beck: Frederick M. Brown/Getty Images; Lady Gaga: Anthony Harvey/Getty Images; P 54-55, Madonna: Mert + Marcus; Water bear: Science Picture/Getty Images; Golden Globe statuette: Chris Haston/NBC; P 57, John and Eminem: Hector Mata/AFP/Getty Images (2); P 59, Perry: Frank Micelotta/PictureGroup; Hanson: Tim Roney/Getty Images; Crow: Terry O›Neill/Hulton Archive/Getty Images; Coldplay: Andreas Rentz/Getty Images; Martin: Miami Herald/Getty Images; Stefani: John Shearer/WireImage; Buffet and Jackson: Scott Gries/Getty Images; Jepsen: Tim Mosenfelder/Getty Images; Shakira: Jeff Kravitz/FilmMagic; Sir Mix-a-Lot: Tim Mosenfelder/Getty Images; Ruiz and Romero: Evan Agostini/Getty Images; P 60-61, McGraw: Gregg DeGuire/WireImage; Underwood, Hill, McBride: Jon Kopaloff/FilmMagic (3); Bryan: Jason Merritt/Getty Images; Brooks: Jason Kempin/ACM2015/Getty

Images; Keith: Frazer Harrison/ACMA2014/Getty Images; Sky: EyeEm/Getty Images; **The Greats Books:** P 62-63, *Harry Potter and the Goblet of Fire*, *The Hunger Games*: Murray Close (2); *Silence of the Lambs*: Ken Regan/Camera 5; *Game of Thrones*: Nick Briggs/HBO; *The Road*: Macall Polay; Child: Lee Lockwood/The LIFE Images Collection/Getty Images; P 64-65, King: Steve Schofield/Contour by Getty Images; Carrie: Marv Newton/MGM/MPTV.net; P 66-67, *The Great Gatsby*: Daniel Smith; John Adams: Kent Eanes/HBO; *The Perks of Being a Wallflower*: John Bramley; *Lord of the Rings: The Two Towers*: Pierre Vinet; *Devil Wears Prada*: Brigitte Lacombe; *Winter's Bone*: Sebastian Mlynarski; *Never Let Me Go*: Alex Bailey; *The Girl With the Dragon Tattoo*: Jean Baptiste Mondino; *Chronicles of Narnia: The Lion, the Witch and the Wardrobe*: Phil Bray; P 68-69, *Jurassic Park*: © Universal City Studios, Inc. & Amblin Entertainment, Inc.; *The Shawshank Redemption*: Michael Weinstein; *Brokeback Mountain*: Kimberly French; *No Country for Old Men*: Richard Foreman; *Gone Girl*, *L.A. Confidential*: Merrick Morton (2); *The Walking Dead*: Gene Page/AMC; *The Golden Compass*: Laurie Sparham; *Eat, Pray, Love*: Francois Duhamel; *Into the Wild*: Chuck Zlotnick; **The Greats YA Novels:** P 71, *The Hunger Games: Catching Fire*: Tim Palen; P 72-73, Green: Ton Koene; Green brothers: Elyse Marshall; Liverpool F.C.: Laurence Griffiths/Getty Images; Vidcon: Jerod Harris/WireImage.

Chapter 2
P 74, Fallon: James White/NBC;

Frozen: © Disney; Jackson: Linda R. Chen; Reeves: Melinda Sue Gordon; *Toy Story 3*: © Disney/Pixar; Depp: Anthony Mandler; Fey: Art Streiber/NBC; *The Lion King*: © Disney; Colbert: Martin Crook/PBS; **Character Studies Superheroes:** P 76-77, *The Amazing Spider-Man* cover: Jack Kirby and Steve Ditko/Copyright © 1962 Marvel Comics; *Iron Man 2*: Michael Muller; *The Office*: Justin Lubin/NBC; *Breaking Bad*: AMC; *Shrek Forever After*: © Dreamworks; P 78-79, *Batman Begins*: Warner Bros.; *Prison Break*: Chuck Hodes/FOX; *Nixon*: Sidney Baldwin; *West Wing*: James Sorensen/NBC; *John Adams*: Kent Eanes/HBO; *Dick*: Columbia/Everett Collection; *Veep*: Patrick Harbron/HBO; *Night at the Museum*: Doane Gregory; P 80-81, *The Flash* cover: Courtesy DC Entertainment; *Empire*: Michael Lavine/FOX; *Pretty Woman*: Ron Batzdorff; *Friends*: NBCU Photo Bank/Getty Images; *Titanic*: Merie Weismuller Wallace; *Downton Abbey*: Nick Briggs/PBS; *The Notebook*: Melissa Moseley; *Castle*: Eric McCandless/ABC; *Scandal*: Michael Ansell/ABC; *Grey's Anatomy*: Danny Feld/ABC; *Brokeback Mountain*: Kimberly French; P 83-83, *X-Men Origins: Wolverine*: Michael Muller; *Incredibles*: Pixar/Disney; *The Fantastic Four* cover: Marvel Entertainment; **Character Studies Villains:** P 84-85, *The Dark Knight*: Stephen Vaughan; *Misery*: Columbia/Everett Collection; *101 Dalmatians*: Walt Disney/Photofest; P 86-87, *Game of Thrones*: Helen Sloan/HBO; *Blade: Trinity*: Diyah Pera; *The Vampire Diaries*: Nino Munoz/CW; *Angel*: Frank Ockenfels/WB; *Dark Shadows*:

Mary Ellen Mark; *The Twilight Saga: Eclipse*: Kimberley French; *True Blood*: John P. Johnson/HBO; *Queen of the Damned*: Warner Bros/Everett Collection; *Bram Stoker's Dracula*: Columbia/Everett Collection; P 88-89, *The Lion King*: Buena Vista/Everett Collection; *Star Trek: First Contact*: Paramount/Everett Collection; *The Walking Dead*: Gene Page/AMC; P 90-91, *Basic Instinct*: Photofest; *Gone Girl*: Merrick Morton; *X-Men: Last Stand*: Nels Israelson; *Game of Thrones*: Paul Schiraldi/HBO; *Kill Bill: Vol. 1*: Andrew Cooper; *The Last Seduction*: Paramount/Everett Collection; *Sons of Anarchy*: Timothy White/FX;

Character Studies Funniest People: P 92-93, Louis-Dreyfus: Gavin Bond/BAFTA Brit 2014/Contour by Getty Images; Rock: Ricardo DeAratanha/Los Angeles Times/Contour by Getty Images; *Downton Abbey*: Nick Briggs/PBS; *The Sopranos*: Barry Wetcher/HBO; *24*: Isabella Vosmikova/FOX; P 94-95, *Seinfeld*: NBC/NBCU Photo Bank via Getty Images; *Saturday Night Live*: Mary Ellen Matthews/NBC/NBCU Photo Bank/Getty Images; Emmy statuette: Getty Images; Comedian: New Material/Miramax/Kobal Collection; P 96-97, Fey: Art Streiber/NBC; Samberg and Timberlake, Fey and Poehler, Hader and Meyers, Wiig and Forte: Dana Edelson/NBC (4); Farley: NBC/NBCU Photo Bank via Getty Images; Shannon: Everett Collection; Myers and Carvey, Sweeney: Alan Singer/NBCU Photo Bank/Getty Images (2); Sandler: Norman Ng/NBC/NBCU Photo Bank via Getty Images; Franken: Al Levine/NBC/NBCU Photo Bank via Getty Images; P 99, Schumer:

Peter Yang/Comedy Central; P 100-101, *Archer*: FX; 24: Kelsey McNeal/FOX; *Covert Affairs*: Christos Kalohoridis/USA Network; *Mission: Impossible*: Paramount/Everett Collection; *The Lives of Others*: Sony/Everett Collection; *Zero Dark Thirty*: Jonathan Olley; *Skyfall*: Francois Duhamel; *Austin Powers: International Man of Mystery*: New Line/Everett Collection; **Character Studies Transformations:** P 102-103, *The Hours*: Clive Coote; *Boys Don't Cry*: Fox Searchlight/Photofest; *The Theory of Everything*: Liam Daniel; *Anchorman 2: The Legend Continues*: Gemma LaMana; P 104-105, *Monk*: Carin Baer/USA; *Lethal Weapon 4*: Warner Bros/Everett Collection; *Poirot*: Everett Collection; *Veronica Mars*: Warner Bros/Everett Collection; *Fargo*: Michael Tackett; *Sherlock*: Robert Viglasky/Hartswood Films for Masterpiece; *Law & Order: Special Victims Unit*: Justin Stephens/NBC; *No. 1 Ladies' Detective Agency*: Nick Wall/HBO; *Homicide: Life on the Street*: Chris Haston/NBC; *Prime Suspect: The Final Act*: PBS; P 106-107, *The Informant!*: Claudette Barius; *Bullets Over Broadway*: Paramount/Everett Collection; *Goodfellas*: Warner Bros/Everett Collection; *Donnie Brasco*: TriStar/Everett Collection; *The Sopranos*: Craig Blankenhorn/HBO; *Pulp Fiction*: Mary Evans/Ronald Grant/Everett Collection; *Road to Perdition*: DreamWorks/Everett Collection; *Analyze This*: Warner Bros/Everett Collection; *Bugsy*: Peter Sorel; *The Simpsons*: FOX; *Breaking Bad*: AMC; P 108-109, Oscar Statuette: Albert Watson; Oscar (r) Statuette © A.M.P.A.S. (r); Skunk: Tom

Brakefield/Getty Images; *Goose: Life on White*/Getty Images; Golden Globe Award: Courtesy of the Hollywood Foreign Press Association; *X-Men: Last Stand*: Nels Israelson; Snoop Dogg: Prince Williams/WireImage; *Terminator 2: Judgement Day*: Everett Collection; P 110-111, Cast Away: Zade Rosenthal; *Guardians of the Galaxy*: © Marvel 2014; *The Addams Family*: Mary Evans/Ronald Grant/Everett Collection; *The Sixth Sense*: Ron Phillips; *Beasts of the Southern Wild*: Ben Richardson; *Interview With the Vampire*: Warner Bros/Everett Collection; *What's Eating Gilbert Grape*: Paramount/Everett Collection; **Character Studies Animation:** P 112-113, *Beauty and the Beast*: Buena Vista/Everett Collection; *Princess Mononoke*: Miramax/Everett Collection; P 114-115, *Toy Story 3*, Incredibles: © Disney/Pixar (2); South Park: Comedy Central.

Chapter 3
P 116, Radcliffe: Peter Mountain; *Cast Away*: Francois Duhamel; Tennant: Adrian Rogers/BBC; *Sherlock*: Robert Viglasky/Hartswood Films for Masterpiece; Big Hero 6: © Disney; Gurira: Gene Page/AMC; Williams: Nicole Rivelli/HBO; **Story Elements Steamiest Moments:** P 119, *Mr. and Mrs. Smith*: Stephen Vaughn; *How to Lose a Guy in 10 Days*: John Clifford; *Deliver Us From Eva*: Jim Sheldon; P 121, *The 40-Year-Old Virgin*: Universal/Everett Collection; *Pretty Woman*: Buena Vista/Photofest; *Brokeback Mountain*: Focus Features/Photofest; *Stranger Than Fiction*: Ralph Nelson; P 123, *Ghost*: Paramount/Everett Collection; *True Blood*: Jaimie

Trueblood/HBO; *Titanic*: Merie W. Wallace; P 125, *Chaplin*: Carolco/Canal/RCS Video/Kobal Collection; *The Player*: Spelling Films/Kobal Collection; *Saving Mr. Banks*: Francois Duhamel; *Morning Glory*: Macall Polay; *Crazy Heart*: Lorey Sebastian; *Dreamgirls*: David James; P 127, *Game of Thrones*: Helen Sloan/HBO; *Sex and the City*: James Devaney/WireImage; Bones: Patrick McElhenney/FOX; *Betsy's Wedding*: Walt Disney/Everett Collection; *Modern Family*: Peter "Hopper" Stone/ABC; *Muriel's Wedding*: Mary Evans/Miramax/Ronald Grant/Everett Collection; *My Big Fat Greek Wedding*: Sophie Giraud; *Outlander*: Neil Davidson/Starz; **Story Elements Late Night Comedy Moments:** P 128-129, *The Tonight Show Starring Jimmy Fallon*: Douglas Gorenstein/NBC/NBCU Photo Bank via Getty Images; *Independence Day*: Claudette Barius; P 130-131, Colbert: Gillian Laub/Contour by Getty Images; Emmy statuette: Getty Images; *AmeriCone Dream*: Jason DeCrow/AP Images; P 132-133, Stewart: Comedy Central; *Late Show With David Letterman*: Alan Singer/CBS/Landov; *The Nanny*: Columbia/MPTV.net; *2 Broke Girls*: Yu Tsai/CBS; P 134, Reed Saxon/AP Images; P 136-137, *Last Week Tonight With John Oliver*: HBO; *Braveheart*, *Kill Bill: Vol. 1*: Andrew Cooper (2); *Sons of Anarchy*: Prashant Gupta/FX; *Game of Thrones*: Helen Sloan/HBO; *Thelma & Louise*: Roland Neveu/MPTV.net; *Fargo*: Gramercy/Everett Collection; *The Wire*: Nicole Rivelli/HBO; *House of Cards*: Nathaniel Bell/Netflix; *Seinfeld*: Gary Null/NBC/NBCU Photo Bank via Getty Images;

Story Elements Special Effects: P 138-139, *Terminator 2: Judgment Day*: TriStar/Everett Collection; *Jurassic Park*: Mary Evans/Everett Collection; *Austin Powers: The Spy Who Shagged Me*: Everett Collection; *Summer of Sam*: Buena Vista/Everett Collection; P 140-141, Cameron: Nic Walker/Fairfax Media/Contour by Getty Images; Oscar statuette: Albert Watson/Oscar (r) Statuette © A.M.P.A.S. (r); *The Terminator*: Orion/Everett Collection; Razzie award: Courtesy of the Razzies; *Titanic*: Merie W. Wallace; Pristimantis james-cameroni: Dr. Philippe Kok; P 142-143, *Lord of the Rings: The Return of the King*: New Line; *Empire*: Michael Lavine/FOX; *The Grifters*: Miramax/Everett Collection; Gold frame: C Squared Studios/Getty Images (2); P 144, *Avatar*: WETA; P 145, *Bourne Supremacy*: Jasin Boland; *Goldeneye*: United Artists/Everett Collection; *Men in Black II*: Melinda Sue Gordon; *Lord of the Rings: The Return of the King*: Pierre Vinet; *Addams Family Values*: Mary Evans/Ronald Grant/Everett Collection; P 146-147, *Baby*: Wolfgang Poelzer/Getty Images; *Elysium*: Stephanie Blomkamp; *Mars*: World Perspectives/Getty Images; *Total Recall*: David Appleby; *Moon, Sky*: EyeEm/Getty Images (2); *Apollo 13*: Universal/Everett Collection; *Doctor Who*: Adrian Rogers/BBC; *Firefly*: FOX; **Story Elements Dystopias:** P 149, *Twelve Monkeys*: Phillip Caruso; P 151, *Lost*: Mario Perez/ABC; *How I Met Your Mother*: Ron P. Jaffe/CBS; *Glee*: Tyler Golden/FOX; *Newhart*: CBS/Landov; *The Office*: Chris Haston/NBC; *Seinfeld*: Joseph Del Valle/NBCU Photo Bank; *Roseanne*: Carsey-Werner/Everett Collection; *The Sopranos*: Will Hart/HBO; *30 Rock*: Ali

Goldstein/NBC; *Buffy The Vampire Slayer*: 20th Century Fox/Everett Collection; P 152-153, *Falling Skies*: TNT/Everett Collection; 300: Warner Bros.; *The Last of the Mohicans*: 20th Century Fox/Everett Collection; *Gettysburg*: New Line/Everett Collection; *Black Hawk Down*: Sydney Baldwin; *The Hurt Locker*: Jonathan Olley; *Starship Troopers*: TriStar/Everett Collection.

Chapter 4

P 154, Gunn: Virginia Sherwood/Bravo; Henson: Michael Lavine/FOX; Polizzi: MTV; Kaling: Emily Shur/FOX; Probst: Robert Voets/CBS; Kardashian: Anders Overgaard/E!; Silverstone: Elliott Marks; Smith: Nick Briggs/PBS; Alexander: Eric Liebowitz/CW; **It's Been Real Reality Stars:** P 156-157, Siriano: Virginia Sherwood/Bravo; Banks: John P. Filo/UPN; P 159, Trump: Virginia Sherwood/NBC; Hatch: Monty Brinton/CBS; Colicchio: Carin Baer/Bravo; *Keeping Up With the Kardashians*: Timothy White/E!; Levine: Trae Patton/NBC; Robertson: Art Streiber; *Jersey Shore*: Scott Gries/MTV; Leakes: Alex Martinez/Bravo; P 160-161, *Dancing With the Stars*: Adam Taylor/ABC; Malakar: Frank Micelotta/FOX; Boyle: Ken McKay/Rex USA; Green: Tyler Golden/NBC/NBCU Photo Bank via Getty Images; P 162-163, Cash: Michael Putland/Retna UK; Barrymore: 20th Century Fox/Everett Collection; Cher: Jeff Kravitz/FilmMagic; Downey Jr.: Zade Rosenthal; Lange: Robert Zuckerman/FX; Brooks: Rick Kern/WireImage; Degeneres: Michael Rozman/Warner Bros.; Sade: Kevin Mazur/Intel/WireImage; **It's Been Real Fashion Moments That Changed Entertainment:** P 165, Lopez: Scott Gries/Getty

Images; Bjork: Vinnie Zuffante/Getty Images; *Mad Men*: Frank Ockenfels 3/AMC; *The Mindy Project*: Isabella Vosmikova/FOX; P 166-167, *Ally McBeal*: Larry Watson/FOX; *The Matrix*: Warner Bros/Kobal Collection; *Clueless*: Elliott Marks; *March Of The Penguins*: Jerome Maison; *Spellbound*: Blitz/Welch/Kobal Collection; *Paris Is Burning*: Michel Compte; *An Inconvenient Truth*: Eric Lee; P 168-169, Wahlberg: Barry King/WireImage; Rihanna: Jeff Kravitz/FilmMagic; Maddox: Matt Cardy/Getty Images; *Beverly Hills, 90210*: FOX; *The Social Network*: Merrick Morton; *Dreamgirls*: David James; *Empire*: Matt Dinnerstein/FOX; **It's Been Real Award-Show Moments:** P 170-171, Spears: Gary Hershorn/Reuters/Corbis; West and Swift: Brad Barket/AP Images; P 172-173, Simpson: Myung J. Chun/AP Images; Clintons: CBS/Landov; US Airways: Bebeto Matthews/AP Images; Palin and Couric: CBS News; Jenner: ABC News; Palance: Reuters/Corbis; DeGeneres selfie: Ellen DeGeneres/Twitter via Getty Images; P 174-175, Winfrey: Art Streiber/OWN; Emmy Statuette: Getty Images; Carter: Library of Congress/MCT/Getty Images; G.H. Bush: Probst/ullstein bild/Getty Images; Clinton: William Philpott/Getty Images; G.W. Bush: Christy Bowe/IPOL/Globe Photos; Obama: Michael Kovac/WireImage; Lady Gaga: Jon Kopaloff/FilmMagic; P 176-177, Etheridge: Michael Caulfield/WireImage; Thicke and Cyrus: Jeff Kravitz/FilmMagic; Dylan: Kevin Mazur/WireImage; **It's Been Real Tech Innovations:** P 178-179, Cat: ICanHascheezburger.com; Controller: Courtesy of Sony; *The Lawnmower Man*: New Line/Everett Collection.

ENTERTAINMENT WEEKLY

Editorial Director Jess Cagle
Editor Henry Goldblatt
Design Director Tim Leong
Photography Director Lisa Berman

EW THE MUST LIST

Editor Alyssa Smith
Project Editor/Writer Katherine Heintzelman
Editor, People + EW Books Allison Adato
Editorial Consultant Erik Forrest Jackson
Art Director Gary Stewart
Interior and Cover Design Michael Picon
Photo Editor Kristine Chin
Writers Darren Franich, Thom Geier, Kevin O'Donnell
Copy Editor Rose Kaplan
Fact Checkers Elizabeth Bland, David Bjerklie, Amy Goehner
Scanners Brien Foy, Salvatore Lopez, Maya Collins
Premedia Executive Director Richard Prue
Senior Manager Romeo Cifelli
Manager Rob Roszkowski
Imaging Production Associate Jennifer Brown
Research Director Céline Wojtala

Time Inc. Books

Publisher Margot Schupf
Associate Publisher Allison Devlin
Vice President, Finance Terri Lombardi
Executive Director, Marketing Services Carol Pittard
Executive Director, Business Development Suzanne Albert
Executive Publishing Director Megan Pearlman
Associate Director of Publicity Courtney Greenhalgh
Assistant General Counsel Andrew Goldberg
Assistant Director, Special Sales Ilene Schreiber
Assistant Director, Finance Christine Font
Assistant Director, Production Susan Chodakiewicz
Senior Manager, Sales Marketing Danielle Costa
Senior Manager, Category Marketing Amanda Lipnick
Associate Prepress Manager Alex Voznesenskiy
Assistant Project Manager Hillary Leary

Editorial Director Stephen Koepp
Art Director Gary Stewart
Editorial Operations Director Jamie Roth Major
Senior Editor Alyssa Smith
Copy Chief Rina Bander
Design Manager Anne-Michelle Gallero
Assistant Managing Editor Gina Scauzillo
Editorial Assistant Courtney Mifsud

SPECIAL THANKS

Allyson Angle, Brad Beatson, Jeremy Biloon, Ian Chin, Rose Cirrincione, Pat Datta, Alison Foster, Erika Hawxhurst, Kristina Jutzi, David Kahn, Jean Kennedy, Seniqua Koger, Amy Mangus, Melissa Presti, Kate Roncinske, Babette Ross, Dave Rozzelle, Divyam Shrivastava, Larry Wicker

ISBN 10: 1-61893-156-3
ISBN 13: 978-1-61893-156-6
Library of Congress Control Number: 2015943627

We welcome your comments and suggestions about Time Inc. Books. Please write to us at: Time Inc. Books, Attention: Book Editors, P.O. Box 361095, Des Moines, IA 50336-1095 If you would like to order any of our hardcover Collector's Edition books, please call us at 800-327-6388, Monday through Friday, 7 a.m.-9 p.m. Central Time.